ASTROSTYLE

The AstroTwins'

2018
Planetary
Planner

CREDITS

Copy Editors: Amy Anthony, Lisa M. Sundry
Assistant Editor: Melissa Gonzales
Contributing Editor: Suzanne Gerber
Cover Photographs: Seher
Zodiac Illustrations © 2018 by Yoko Furusho
Design: We Are Branch, wearebranch.com

"Treat the Earth well.

It was not given to you by your parents,

It was loaned to you by your children.

We do not inherit the Earth from our ancestors,

We borrow it from our children."

—*Native American Proverb*

2018

A MESSAGE FROM The AstroTwins

Dear Reader,

As professional astrologers, we've been tracking the stars for over 20 years. We've prosecuted Pluto for pulling us into the shadows, slammed Saturn for suppressing our *joie de vivre*. But at this moment in history, it seems that we're living on the most high-maintenance planet in the solar system: Mother freakin' Earth. As above, so below? Um, not with this much "mama drama."

Every year, we reserve this page so we can attempt to encapsulate an overriding theme for the year ahead, to make sense of the cosmic curveballs in a few short paragraphs. But blanket statements just won't do now.

In 2018, there isn't one simple, uplifting message that summarizes the entire year—nor is there one that makes sense of the past couple years. We've started drafts about the need to come together in a time of polarized politics. About how we can acknowledge our differences without growing more divided and separate. But it all either sounded too cliché, too *kumbaya*—or just apocalyptic and depressing.

One thread was about 2018 being an 11/2 Universal Year in numerology, which is all about balancing individuality and partnership. Certainly, this duality is real. Friendships and family ties have been frayed by elections, social media and stomach-churning headlines. We ourselves can start the day in awe of the human spirit, only to plunge into a judgmental funk by sundown, thinking, "people suck" or "the world is doomed." More than ever, we feel so lucky to have the tools of astrology to help us shake that off.

Here's our semi-conclusion: Sometimes, the stars don't hand us easy solutions. They offer us rough guidance. Clues. A trail to investigate.

The stars are as much our teachers as they are our guides—the ones that send us home with a hard assignment and push us to look deeper. Sometimes, they give us more questions than answers. Sometimes, they speak to us in code.

In spite of all this heaviness, there actually *is* a lot to look forward to in 2018. And there are also hard choices, sharp turns and adjustments—as you'll read about in the coming pages.

Rather than being mere passengers on this mothership, it's time for us to become captains and cruise directors. We must learn to navigate (the stars have always been a great compass) and stay afloat. But we might as well sing some karaoke on the lido deck and hit the seafood buffet while we're all trapped in the middle of this vast existential ocean. The human spirit can't survive without levity, even when everything around us seems blanketed in fog.

It seems we're still between ports, and the ride has been choppy, storm-filled and as enigmatic as the Loch Ness Monster. In 2018, we'll keep learning how to seize the wheel and steer ourselves to safe harbor—or perhaps, to a brave new world. All hands on deck?

Ophira & Tali

Ophira & Tali Edut
The AstroTwins

Table of Contents

2018 Cosmic Overview

What's in the Stars for All of Us?

Could sweet stability be in the stars in 2018? We're cautiously optimistic, given the last few years of cosmic chaos. But a peek upstairs reveals a little more quiet than we've had in the past few years.

By November, three planets (Jupiter, Saturn and Neptune) will be rooted in their "home" signs—meaning they will travel through the zodiac sign that they govern—a cycle that will last until December 2019.

Effusive Jupiter will be in its native Sagittarius from November 8, 2018 until December 2, 2019; staunch Saturn is anchored in Capricorn until December 2020 and watery Neptune is in Pisces until 2024.

This is like getting a double-strength dose of what each planet rules: Jupiter's optimism, Saturn's pragmatism and Neptune's compassion. Planets are happiest in their own domains, so here's hoping we feel their alignment down here on Earth.

Jupiter in Scorpio & Sagittarius: Redefining power.

Jupiter reveals where humanity will expand, take risks and evolve. Since it changes signs every 12 to 13 months, the spotted planet plays a huge hand in shaping the mood of each year.

Last year, Jupiter was in Libra, the sign of justice and balance. Jupiter rules cross-cultural and international relations, media, travel and higher education. We saw major shifts in global power and attacks on journalism's credibility with "fake news" and "alternative facts." Unjust travel bans made headlines—and ignited multiple lawsuits against the government. There were also record numbers of peaceful (Libra) protests, like the historic Women's Marches around the globe and the airport rallies to decry the attempted "Muslim ban."

In 2018, the little things matter—a lot! Big-picture Jupiter will be in micro-focused Scorpio until November 8, training our attention on the details. Themes of life and death, real estate, long-term finances, sex and power fall under Scorpio's domain. Russia, North Korea, the European Union, the United States: Changing alliances will further reshuffle the global power structures. With truth-telling Jupiter in secretive Scorpio, we can expect more leaks and shocking reveals of "classified" information.

When Jupiter returns home to Sagittarius on November 8, international issues will take the spotlight. This entrepreneurial energy will also be a boon for startups and solopreneurs, as we'll all crave more freedom. Travel, publishing and multicultural relationships will also be hot-button topics. Moving from Scorpio to Sagittarius is like changing your viewfinder from detail-focus to wide-angle. We'll emerge from the intense depths and focus on broader, more worldly topics.

Work & money in 2018: Jupiter, Saturn, Uranus & Pluto step in.

Get ready—the economy is going to go through some serious reforms in 2018. Several of the outer planets will travel through signs related to finance, power, corporations and shared resources, shifting the way business is conducted in some fundamental ways.

Structured Saturn and shadowy Pluto will both spend the year in patriarchal Capricorn, ruler of big business, banks, the government and hierarchy. Saturn is here until December 2020, while transformational Pluto is touring Capricorn from 2008 to 2024. As these planetary power players inch along in the same sign, we may see a rise in monopolies but also a crackdown on scandals. Saturn is the "integrity cop" of the cosmos, exposing shady business.

This year may also bring leaner times and corporate cutbacks. However, old-school Saturn in hardworking Capricorn could revive a bootstrapping work ethic. Will all of those promised manufacturing jobs return to the United States?

We'll find out in 2018. The Great Depression occurred while Saturn was in Capricorn from 1929 to 1932, and here's hoping that we learn from the mistakes of yesteryear and keep our expectations—along with the stock market—grounded in reality.

Meanwhile, generous Jupiter hovers in Scorpio, the sign of joint ventures, mergers and pooled resources, until November. The sharing economy may boom, possibly out of necessity, as people look for creative ways to consolidate and cut costs. Real estate and lending is ruled by Scorpio. Housing prices could soar, making it a seller's market. But with over-the-top Jupiter, the bubble might burst—and Scorpio's influence could bring some sketchy deals back to market. From balloon mortgages to "no money down" loans, home buyers should be careful not to get in over their heads or repeat the mistakes of the 2008 crash.

Economic reform could be in the stars as revolutionary Uranus enters Taurus, the sign of money and daily work, for the first time since 1942! The side-spinning planet visits each sign for seven years, and it will be here from May 15, 2018 until April 2026. Unpredictable Uranus will shake up business as usual, revamping the way we spend, earn, save and invest. Innovation and technology will play a role—for example, we may see the rise of "cashless" businesses and the growing automation of Artificial Intelligence (AI) replacing human

> "Economic reform could be in the stars as revolutionary Uranus enters Taurus, the sign of money and daily work, for the first time since 1942, revamping the way we spend, save and invest."

labor. Uranus was in Taurus during the 1850s Gold Rush and again from 1934-42, a historical era that included the Great Depression and World War II, but also the Social Security and unemployment policies that are in effect to this day.

Neptune in Pisces: Artistic & spiritual renaissance.

Countering all of this money and work-driven energy, dreamy Neptune continues floating through its home sign of Pisces from 2012 to 2026. Neptune's touch is evident in the booming wellness movement. Yoga, meditation, crystals, retreats—all things "woo" have become decidedly mainstream as Neptune nears the halfway point of its journey. (Anyone for a $14 cold-pressed, gem-infused juice brewed with activated charcoal?) Creative, compassionate Neptune champions the arts and spurs social activism. The shadow expression of Neptune is secrecy and illusion. From brewing political scandals to genocide to ISIS, this cycle has also exposed some hidden horrors in the world.

Jupiter-Neptune Trine: Global healing and compassion.

Could peace finally come to our world—at least, in some small way? An awakening of higher consciousness and compassion might arise this spring, when cross-cultural ambassador Jupiter unites in a langorous and harmonious trine (120-degree angle) with soul-stirring Neptune in May of 2018. The duo will both be traveling through emotional and receptive water signs (Jupiter in Scorpio and Neptune in Pisces) most of the year, opening our hearts.

The exact trine will culminate on May 25, but they'll be in close contact from May until August. This rare and unifying cycle reminds us that, while we may be "divided" by cultures and nations, we are all one. This could be a banner moment for love, with merging-minded Scorpio and starry-eyed Pisces in the mix. Don't be surprised if you get more than your usual share of engagement or "we're expecting!" announcements. But Jupiter and Neptune are freedom-lovers at heart. You can be sure that any news will come with an unconventional twist. ("Surprise! Our son was born via natural hypnobirthing in a yurt and we're moving abroad to raise him on a collective farm." Not that there's anything wrong with that.)

Water, water everywhere—and not a drop to drink? On an international level, headlines could center on the global water crisis and the climate effects of rising temperatures. As polar ice caps melted, record high temperatures last winter caused unprecedented greenery to grow in both the North and South poles. Huge swaths of the world lives without clean water. Recent statistics from Water.org show that one in ten people (663 million) lack

 The AstroTwins' 2018 Gemini Planetary Planner

access to safe drinking water and 2.4 billion don't have proper sanitation. Since abundant Jupiter magnifies whatever it touches and Neptune rules the seas, we may see an ocean-related weather surge near these dates.

Since 2012, the outer planets have been making a series of challenging aspects (angles), which has shaken up business as usual. Since the large, slow-moving outer planets shape generational and global trends, everything from politics to culture has been impacted. This is the first time in over five years that we won't experience any major battles between these cosmic players.

Jupiter and Neptune last made contact when they locked into a tense and heated opposition from August until October of 2015, then again from March until July of 2016. Their exact faceoff was mid-September 2015, but the effect could be felt during these whole periods. At the time, Jupiter was in analytical Virgo, an odd contrast to artsy, spiritual Neptune. Complicating matters, restrictive Saturn (in global Sagittarius) wedged itself in the middle, forming a tense and awkward T-square.

Many people will recall 2015 and 2016 as especially tough years, and the Jupiter-Neptune-Saturn conflicts only fueled this intensity. There was also a series of harsh angles between Jupiter, revolutionary Uranus and shadowy Pluto in 2016 and 2017. These erupted in chaos and confusion, especially on the political stage. Global alliances reshuffled—with conflict coming from every angle, and primarily involving the Middle East, North Korea, Russia and the United States. With Jupiter

coursing through potent Scorpio until November 2018, we can expect more changes among the powers that be.

Love, sex & relationships in 2018: Privacy please!

Feisty Jupiter is in Scorpio, ruler of sex and intimacy, from October 10, 2017 until November 8, 2018. While outspoken Jupiter might awaken some evolved attitudes about love and sexuality, it can also spread some less savory stuff (like new strains of STDs). On the other hand, progressive Jupiter, which rules publishing and higher learning, could help reform outdated sex education programs. We might see students learn not just about how babies are made but also how to dismantle gender stereotyping, protect privacy in the age of Snapchat and sexting, and battle the pervasive rape culture. Scorpio rules the psyche, so understanding human behavior and motivations could make a huge difference in safe, consensual enjoyment of our bodies and sexuality.

In November, Jupiter will enter try-anything-once Sagittarius, offering up plenty of willing playmates who are eager to turn those Scorpio-fueled fantasies into reality. Open-minded Sagittarius is all about loving across so-called boundaries in gender, race or religion. Long-distance love could move beyond time-zone-crossing WhatsApp chats, as global Jupiter in Sagittarius brings new ways to connect. With Jupiter in this dishy sign, conversations may come with a TMI alert, as people share explicitly and unapologetically about their escapades. (There's a reason the Parental Advisory sticker was invented a year after Jupiter left Sagittarius!)

8

With Saturn in conservative Capricorn, we may see an uptick in more traditional relationships running parallel to (and perhaps in response to) these Jupiter trends. Promise ring, anyone? In other cases, Saturn's suppressive effect will find outdated institutions crumbling as people lose their taste for exclusionary and irrelevant customs. Since Saturn rules aging, we may see a rise in weddings or vow renewals among older people—a spike in Boomer brides, perhaps?

Fashion, decor & style in 2018: Teased, tatted...and tailored.

Smoky eyes, seductive silhouettes, lingerie-inspired styles...fashion takes a turn for the smoldering with Jupiter in sexy Scorpio until November 8. Paging Madonna circa 1992! Designers might take inspiration from burlesque, pin-up—even bondage, creating looks designed to make a statement about

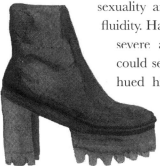

sexuality and its ever-increasing fluidity. Hairstyles may get sleek, severe and choppy, and we could see a turn from honey-hued highlights and cotton-candy dye to inky blacks and navys.

Mysticism and other "hidden" or underground scenes could also weave their way in. Interior design could also adopt a heavy, incense-laden boudoir or fortune-teller influence. Scorpio could bring back black leather dresses with corsetry or elaborate getups that take time and effort to put on. With detail-loving Scorpio as stylist, custom, limited-edition and "small-batch" lines could also do well. Instead of fast fashion, we might want hand-engraved and artisan pieces with a rich story behind them.

When Jupiter moves into larger-than-life Sagittarius for 13 months on November 8, styles will shift from exclusive to over-the-top. We'll want comfort, personality and fun clothing that makes an undeniable statement. Decorating could also trend toward colorful and international now, with oversized furniture and statement pieces making a comeback. Exaggerated details and eye-popping colors will return.

When Jupiter visited hedonistic Sagittarius in 1995, we got the campy, colorful movie *Clueless* and its shop-'til-you-drop ethos, and Jupiter's 1983 tour of Sagittarius introduced shoulder pads, roomy parachute pants, wild-patterned Swatch watches and multi-hued jelly shoes. This Jupiter cycle also brought the roots of athleisure and street style, unleashing a wave of leg warmers, headbands and Spandex leggings to coincide with the aerobics and breakdancing crazes. Slouchy, off-the-shoulder sweatshirts (inspired by the movie *Flashdance*) were everywhere, and Madonna's "Lucky Star" video put mesh crop tops, giant hair bows and lace gloves on every girl's wishlist. By the end of 2018, we'll want clothing that frees, rather than binds, because this transit will have us on the move!

Running parallel to these trends, as structured Saturn returns to its regimented home sign of Capricorn all year, military-inspired looks could also make their way back into the zeitgeist. Brass buttons, tailored trenches, epaulets and patches could pair with heavy boots—or hiking ones, since Capricorn is symbolized by the mountain goat. The concept of "uniform" dressing may take hold, as busy people seek ways to look stylish without losing billable hours. Interestingly, Saturn's last visit to Capricorn from 1989 to 1991 coincided with a recession and the need for practicality. The preeminent staple of these years was the jacket. Blazers were teamed with everything: T-shirts and leggings, jeans and shorts, skirts of all lengths. A well-made blazer might be your Saturn in Capricorn essential. Mix it with a corset, a babydoll dress or oversized "Hammer pants"—use Jupiter (and your own judgment) as your stylist!

Health & wellness: From research to reincarnation.

Pioneering discoveries will make headlines as Jupiter deep-dives into inquisitive Scorpio until November 8. This transit may bring breakthroughs in research, especially around diseases spread through infections and the blood. Psychology is also ruled by Scorpio, and new therapy developments could emerge.

Doctors may pioneer cutting-edge cancer treatments or life-extending clinical trials that actually work. With Scorpio's mystical bent, groundbreaking members of the medical field could integrate holistic treatments or "plant medicine" into their practices. Move over, pharmaceuticals—the growing field of psychopharmacology is using magic mushrooms and MDMA to treat cancer-related depression and

PTSD. Could we see an FDA approval with Jupiter in Scorpio? Either way, Jupiter in transformational Scorpio might bring a rise in self-healing that includes energy medicine, microdosing, ayuhuasca and shamanic work.

Scorpio rules birth, death and reincarnation, and during this Jupiter cycle, cutting-edge brain science could emerge about how to slow and even reverse dying. People may work to overcome their fear of death, backed by spirituality and science. The Near Death Experience might become fodder for closer examination. Worldly Jupiter may inspire a closer look at how non-Western cultures treat death as a sacred process. Our own beloved staff member Melissa recently trained to be a "death doula," learning techniques to shepherd people through their transition. Philosophical Jupiter makes us more inquisitive about metaphysical end-of-life options, ones that go beyond dying in hospice or a hospital. Fascination with the afterlife and past lives could also spread, perhaps with new scientific evidence.

Whew! After all this intensity, we're ready to feel alive. On November 8, Jupiter moves into worldly Sagittarius for 13 months. Athletics, outdoor adventures

"Year of the Dog traits include humble service, friendship and kindness—and we could all use a little more of that."

and joie de vivre replace the Scorpionic intensity. Jupiter is the god of the feast, and in its home sign of Sagittarius, excess abounds. Healthy eating will have to feel decadent, bountiful and communal (generous Sagittarius loves to share). International influences will inspire new fusion dishes, and new superfoods will join the ranks of acai and maca. More people may begin growing and farming their own food, and organic neighborhood plots could pop up everywhere with an added focus on preserving soil integrity for growing prime food. Since brainy Sagittarius loves to learn and teach, education around nutrition and fitness will boom. This entrepreneurial transit might also bring a rise in celebrity instructors, coaches and trainers.

Numerology in 2018:
An 11/2 Universal Year.

Come together! After three transitional years, a unifying numerological cycle arrives. The "2" vibration inspires partnership, and this year is especially potent because it also contains the master number "11." Universal years are calculated by adding the digits of the year (in this case 2+0+1+8 = 11; 1+1 = 2). Working together, compromising and choosing high-vibe alliances will be a strong and much-needed theme. That said, 11 is a double vibration of 1, so we can expect another year of rapid-fire change and independence, even as we move toward greater cooperation.

Year of the Earth Dog: Loyalty rules.

Roll over, Rooster—El Bow Wow is in the house. After a year of the fastidious Fire Cock strutting around keeping order, the Year of the Earth Dog begins. Dog energy is playful, happy and loyal.

But to whom does that loyalty belong? Dogs are pack animals who follow a strong and decisive Alpha figure. During this Chinese zodiac cycle, we must be careful not to be seduced by strength alone. Might does not make right, and the Dog Year reminds us not to be obedient followers who succumb to authority. Praise and a pat on the head feel great, but the world needs critical thinking, not blind devotion (or seduction by biscuit).

The Dog is associated with the Western sign of Libra, a lover of beauty and grace. Lavish entertaining and formal events could make a comeback and we may see a renaissance for the design industry. The best traits to emerge from these Dog days will be humble service, friendship and kindness, and we could all use a little more of that! ✳

New & Full Moons in 2018

Manifest and motivate by the moon's phases.

Following moon cycles can be a great way to set goals and reap their benefits. Astrologers believe that our energy awakens at the new moon, then peaks two weeks later at the full moon. In many cultures, farmers have planted by the new moon and harvested by the full moon. Why not get a little lunar boost for your own life?

There is also a six-month buildup between new and full moons. Each new moon falls in a specific zodiac sign. Then, six months later, a full moon occurs in that same zodiac sign.

New moons mark beginnings and are the perfect time to kick off any new projects or idea. Lay the groundwork for what you want to manifest in the coming six months. Set intentions or initiate plans and tend to them for a half year.

Full moons are times for completions, creative outpourings, and harvesting. They're also your cue to cash in on anything you started at the corresponding new moon six months earlier. What have you been building toward? Full moons act as cosmic spotlights, illuminating what's been hidden. It's an opportunity to take stock of your efforts. Don't like the direction things are taking? Change course at the full moon. ✴

2018 New Moons

1/16	Capricorn 9:17pm
2/15	Aquarius (solar eclipse) 4:05pm
3/17	Pisces 9:11am
4/15	Aries 9:57pm
5/15	Taurus 7:47am
6/13	Gemini 3:43pm
7/12	Cancer (solar eclipse) 10:47pm
8/11	Leo (solar eclipse) 5:57am
9/9	Virgo 2:01pm
10/8	Libra 11:46pm
11/7	Scorpio 11:01am
12/7	Sagittarius 2:20am

2018 Full Moons

1/1	Cancer (supermoon) 9:24pm
1/31	Leo (total lunar eclipse/supermoon) 8:26am
3/1	Virgo 7:51am
3/31	Libra 8:36am
4/29	Scorpio 8:58pm
5/29	Sagittarius 10:19am
6/28	Capricorn 12:53am
7/27	Aquarius (total lunar eclipse) 4:20pm
8/26	Pisces 7:56am
9/24	Aries 10:52pm
10/24	Taurus 12:45pm
11/23	Gemini 12:30am
12/22	Cancer 12:48pm

*BASED ON EASTERN STANDARD TIME

Eclipses in 2018

Brace yourself for big changes, plot twists & bold moves.

Eclipses happen four to six times a year, bringing sudden changes and turning points to our lives. If you've been sitting on the fence about an issue, an eclipse forces you to make a decision. Unexpected circumstances arise and demand a radical change of plans. Truths and secrets explode into the open. Things that aren't "meant to be" are swept away without notice. Shocking as their delivery can be, eclipses help open up space for the new.

The ancients used to hide from eclipses and viewed them as omens or bearers of disruptive change. And who could blame them? They planted, hunted, fished and moved by the cycles of nature and the stars. While the modern astrological approach is not fear-based, we must still respect the eclipses' power. We've experienced major events in our own lives: Ophi met her husband Jeffrey on a solar eclipse in 2006, and at last year's Leo total solar eclipse, her beloved 13-year-old dachshund, Seymour, passed away peacefully in his sleep. (Incidentally, Seymour was also born on a solar eclipse in 2004. Talk about a powerful transition!)

There are two types of eclipses—solar and lunar. Lunar eclipses fall at full moons. The earth passes directly between the Sun and the moon, cutting off their communication and casting a shadow on the earth, which often appears in dramatic red and brown shades. A solar eclipse takes place when the new moon passes between the Sun and the earth, shadowing the Sun. The effect is like a spiritual power outage—a solar eclipse either makes you feel wildly off-center, or your mind becomes crystal-clear.

The effects of an eclipse can usually be felt for three to five days before and after the event (some astrologers say eclipses can announce themselves a month before or after, too). Expect the unexpected, and wait for the dust to settle before you act on any eclipse-fueled impulses. ✽

2018 Eclipses

1/31	Total lunar eclipse (Leo)
2/15	Solar eclipse (Aquarius)
7/12	Solar eclipse (Cancer)
7/27	Total lunar eclipse (Aquarius)
8/11	Solar eclipse (Leo)

Retrogrades in 2018

When planets go "backward," slowdowns and chaos can ensue.

You've heard the hype about retrogrades—but what are they, really? When a planet passes the Earth in its journey around the Sun, it's said to be going retrograde. From our vantage point on Earth, it is almost as if the planet is moving in reverse. This is an illusion, but it's a bit like two trains passing at different speeds—one appears to be going backward. When a planet goes retrograde (for a few weeks, or sometimes even months), everything that falls under its jurisdiction can go a bit haywire.

The most commonly discussed retrograde is Mercury retrograde, which happens 3-4 times a year. Mercury rules communication, travel and technology, and these transits are notorious for crashing computers, causing misunderstandings, delaying flights, and even souring deals. Astrologers typically warn against traveling, buying new electronic gadgets or signing legally binding contracts during Mercury retrograde. However, all planets go retrograde at a certain point. Venus reverses course every 18 months; Mars, every two years. The outer planets—Jupiter, Saturn, Uranus, Neptune and Pluto—spend four to five months retrograde every year.

Survival tip: Think of the prefix "re-" when planning the best use of a retrograde. Review, reunite, reconnect, research. Retrogrades aren't the best times to begin something new, but they can be stellar phases for tying up loose ends or giving a stalled mission a second chance. ✸

2018 Retrograde Planets & Dates

MERCURY	MARS	URANUS
March 22–April 15	June 26–August 27	August 7–January 6
July 26–August 19		
November 16–December 6	**JUPITER**	**NEPTUNE**
	March 8–July 10	June 18–November 24
VENUS		
October 5–November 16	**SATURN**	**PLUTO**
	April 17–September 6	April 22–September 30

Jupiter in Scorpio

Jupiter in soulful Scorpio illuminates money, power and mysticism from October 10, 2017 – November 8, 2018.

How deep is your love? Insert for "what" or "whom" here! Ever since Jupiter changed wavelengths from fair-and-balanced Libra into never-to-be-forgotten Scorpio on October 10, 2017, life has gotten more intense. Last year had its share of neck-swiveling moments, to be sure.

We experienced a few crashes and burns on the road to creating some semblance of Libra peace and harmony for most of 2018, we can sit back and watch the mighty Scorpio phoenix rise, as abundant Jupiter plays alchemist, helping us transmute the smoldering ash into pure gold.

Call it…abundance with a (leather) twist. Outspoken Jupiter in enigmatic Scorpio will reach into the depths and broadcast its findings, loud and proud. Jupiter was last in Scorpio from October 25, 2005 until November 23, 2006. Page back and reflect: What similar situations (or actual people) are resurfacing now?

While Jupiter is in mystical and seductive Scorpio, everything is sacred, but the planet of exposure will make it hard to keep anything a secret. In fact, the world could grow fascinated with the esoteric—from unsolved mysteries to the occult to paranormal occurrences. Since Scorpio rules the erotic, we'll want to peek behind those lace-trimmed velvet curtains for a few boudoir hacks, too. From crop circles to riding crops, Jupiter in sexy and spiritual Scorpio will take us there!

Scorpionic themes of life, death, rebirth and s-e-x will occupy universal consciousness. And with global Jupiter here, our search for other life forms could expand. Fun fact: The epic blockbuster *E.T.* debuted in 1982 while Jupiter was in Scorpio, along with Michael Jackson's *Thriller*—an (at the time) unprecedented ten-minute long video featuring zombies creeping from their crypts.

It will be a relief to have optimistic Jupiter here, because from 2012 until 2015, we weathered heavy Saturn lumbering through Scorpio, adding more weightiness to spiritual, emotional and sexual matters.

With adventurous Jupiter touring the sign of mystery, we'll take a lighter and more experimental approach—but also a philosophical

The AstroTwins' 2018 Gemini Planetary Planner

one. Jupiter rules publishing and broadcasting. Books, shows and podcasts dealing with topics of transformation (financial and personal) could gain popularity. With psychological Scorpio at play, we'll all want to pop the hood and see the inner workings.

Fashion & style with Jupiter in Scorpio.

Leather, hardware, bondage or bandage—Jupiter in sultry Scorpio brings us body-con with a dollop of dominatrix. The *Fifty Shades* franchise already took S&M mainstream (making a cloying attempt to romanticize it while Jupiter was in sticky-sweet Libra), but there's room for a resurgence of "power dressing" and lingerie-inspired fashion.

The epic prime-time soap opera *Dynasty* became a television sensation in 1981 during Jupiter's tour of Libra and Scorpio, bringing us embellished jackets, padded shoulders, shiny dresses and the lacy teddy nightgown to pair with scandalous, come-hither "nightcaps." It was the perfect wardrobe for a backdrop of feuding families, lavish wealth, backstabbing, lust and greed—the Scorpionic extremes.

With sporty Jupiter in severe Scorpio, fashion could play up contrast by mixing high and low in innovative ways. A combo of Jimmy Choos (a

Scorpio himself), a vintage Members Only jacket and parachute pants might be surprisingly chic now. Styles meant for the sheets could make their way onto the streets. Move over, athleisure; make way for…athlingerie? Dark sunglasses, spywear, and all-white or all-black could make a comeback. Egalitarian Jupiter in wealth-conscious Scorpio might street-style the custom suit or Wall Street tycoon look.

Sexual liberation: Getting in tune with your soulful sexiness.

Peek-a-boo! Outspoken Jupiter and private Scorpio don't make the most natural of bedfellows, but their pillow talk can be stimulating and spicy nonetheless. Since Jupiter rules higher education, you might take some intellectually *and* erotically stimulating workshops, expanding your boudoir repertoire and learning more about your own sensual nature. Reading up on sexual development may also give you deeper insight into your own carnal desires, since Scorpio rules the psyche. (So that's why you keep falling for that type!) Jupiter is wild but also high-vibe, and this cycle could lend an air of mindfulness to our intimate encounters.

Love & relationships during Jupiter in Scorpio.

Although Scorpio is the sign most associated with sexual exploration and erotica, it is also the natural ruler of the eighth house of soulful mergers.

16

Jupiter's run through marriage-minded Libra may have brought an uptick in back-to-basic merging by way of the traditional vows and contracts. With philosophical Jupiter in Scorpio, one can only swipe for so long or explore sexual positions from so many angles until…well…even that becomes mundane. Under Jupiter's expansive touch, could depth of bond be the new "kinky" in today's social-sexual climate?

Rethinking monogamy?

Deep-diving Scorpio is known for being jealous and possessive, but experimental Jupiter is all about freedom. These energies are a curious mix that could lead to some interesting explorations and philosophical debates. Where is the line between commitment and ownership—and how do we maintain our freedom within a permanent commitment? With Jupiter in Scorpio, we'll explore how we can go deeper in relationships instead of broader. If you're serious about exploring—or even just looking for a new take on monogamy—you might check out a book like *The Ethical Slut*, which addresses the very real issue of jealousy from a more introspective angle. Read up on "compersion," which is the flip side of jealousy: the positive feelings one gets from seeing a love interest enjoy other friends, creative collaborations and (should you dare to dabble) even romantic relationships.

Breakthroughs in disease research, reproductive rights.

Scorpio rules research, and with global Jupiter here, certain infectious and contagious diseases could become pressing world health issues. Since sexuality, bloodwork and reproductive health fall under Scorpio's domain, the Zika virus might become a more widespread health concern. Interestingly, Jupiter was also in Scorpio from late 1981 until late 1982, just as the AIDS crisis took hold. In January 1982, the first-ever AIDS clinic was established in San Francisco. During this cycle, the Gay Men's Health Crisis was founded and the CDC used the term "AIDS" for the first time. We may see inspiring advances in stem cell research or new cures for cancer, particularly lymphoma, leukemia, ovarian and prostate cancer.

On an international level, Jupiter in Scorpio could lend support to women's sexual health and reproductive rights. With Planned Parenthood and *Roe v. Wade* under the gun in the U.S., this cycle could spur another historic Women's March and other forms of activism. Sex trafficking and female genital mutilation are still rampant, including in the U.S. and other modernized nations. Did you know that 1 in 3 girls in developing countries are married before age 18? On top of that, complications during pregnancy are the leading cause of death for 15-19 year-old females globally. Women make up the majority of the world's poorest citizens. Yet, educating girls—which is forbidden in many parts of the world—is one of the keys to ending poverty and creating world peace. With a small microloan, a woman can start or sustain a business in a developing nation. This Jupiter cycle might help girls and women gain access to education, healthcare and economic opportunity.

Financial reform, investing wisely.

Equitable Jupiter in power-player Scorpio could bring highs and lows to financial issues. This may be an abundant time for the stock market, as Jupiter, the cosmic gambler, makes people more willing to take risks with their investments. Caution: Jupiter can also breed overconfidence, so don't turn your Dow Jones dabbling into straight-up gambling. Keep that portfolio diversified with a mix of higher-risk (Jupiter's domain) stocks and safe bet investments like bonds and mutual funds.

Scorpio rules joint ventures, shared assets and "other people's money"—loans, inheritances, royalties, commissions, debt and property ownership could all become hot issues. Jupiter in Scorpio is also a great time to do retirement and estate planning, to build up your savings or to get a living will in order. You might consolidate your debt, cut up your credit cards or look for ways to get tax breaks through charitable giving. Scorpio rules real estate, so this cycle could be a boon for the property market. With housing prices tipping the scales in major U.S. cities, we may see people flocking to develop midsize cities, living more communally or finally bursting the real estate market's bubble.

Truth-teller Jupiter might also expose corruption among the "one percent." The wealthy may have to open up their confidential files and banks could go through scrutiny. Allegations of fraud and Ponzi schemes could dot the headlines. Watch out for network marketing companies that have a pyramid structure. With cocky Jupiter in Scorpio, we might fall for someone's big promises of overnight millions and early retirement. That said, this Jupiter transit could bring legitimate ways of earning passive income through affiliate programs, commissions, royalties and other "shared economy" innovations.

Addiction and recovery.

Scorpio tempts us to live on the edge, and adventure-seeking Jupiter only fans those flames. Be careful with addictive substances and obsessive pursuits, as you could be drawn to danger now. If you're in recovery or battling with a vice, Jupiter in Scorpio demands an "all or nothing" 12-step approach of avoiding the first sip or interaction—no gray shades here. Mental health issues might gain more exposure and understanding during this cycle. It was during Jupiter's 1994 transit of Scorpio that Kurt Cobain committed suicide, having suffered with both heroin addiction and depression. Hopefully, high-minded Jupiter will bring more education and awareness to these widespread struggles.

New outlooks on death & afterlife.

Jupiter in mystical Scorpio piques our interest in the paranormal, life after death and the esoteric realm. Scorpio is associated with death and reincarnation, and if you've lost a loved one, you might find comfort in reading *Many Lives, Many Masters* by Dr. Brian Weiss (a Scorpio himself). You could book a session with a reputable medium or explore the deeper question of "Who am I beyond my body?" While our bodies are finite, atoms and energy never die, so the eternal presence of the "soul" may get deeper scientific support now. Perhaps we'll move beyond sensationalized "ghost hunter" and horror movie stereotypes and gain a deeper understanding of life after death. Some people may even explore ways to have out-of-body experiences, experimenting with sound healing, holotropic breathing or "micro-dosing," or even going all the way to the esoteric realm with a shaman-led ayahuasca ceremony.

Regardless of what actually manifests during this Jupiter in Scorpio transit (at a global or personal level), rest assured: It will anything but routine. Time to dive deep! ✳

Jupiter in Sagittarius

Global connections ignite as Jupiter returns to its home sign from November 8, 2018 – December 2, 2019.

S weet home, Alabama! Or is that Australia, Argentina or Amsterdam? On November 8, 2018, global Jupiter lands in its native sign of Sagittarius for a 13-month visit. Jupiter is the natural ruler of Sagittarius, so we'll get a double dose of expansive and enterprising energy. Bring on the positive thinking and limitless possibilities! A spirit of adventure overtakes us now, and it's such a refreshing change. Ready to take a bold leap of faith? There's nothing Jupiter loves more than a gutsy risk, so strap on your multicolored parachute and jump!

Jupiter's move from myopic Scorpio to big-picture Sagittarius is like adjusting our viewfinders from microscopic detail to a wide-angle setting. We'll emerge from 13 intense and transformational months in the Scorpio cocoon, exiting the chrysalis and spreading our butterfly wings like it's Carnival season in Brazil. What a bright and wonderful world we will see through the optimistic Sagittarius lens! Be sure to soak up the happy-go-lucky vibes while you can—Jupiter only visits each sign every 12 years. Its last tour of Sagittarius was from November 24, 2006, until December 18, 2007. What were you

doing 12 years ago? You may see themes from that time in your life emerge once again.

Cast a wide net! Travel and international friendships.

While Jupiter is in Sagittarius, we're hungry for fresh experiences and mind-expanding ideas. Stretch beyond the familiar! Spin the globe and visit a country that's on your bucket list. Learn a foreign language or engage in philosophical dialogue with people from different cultures and backgrounds. The travel sector could boom during this Jupiter cycle, as new innovations shorten the distance between us and our global neighbors. From high-speed planes and trains to sleek new airports to the next iteration of FaceTime and WhatsApp, time zones will soon be "nothing but a number."

The way we travel could evolve, as it has during past Jupiter in Sagittarius cycles. In 1924, while Jupiter was here, the U.S. Army completed the first-ever 'round the world flight. The inaugural Hindenburg flight was in 1936, during Jupiter's next visit to Sagittarius.

         The AstroTwins' 2018 Gemini Planetary Planner

Where will we go next? With a space race already underway, the first "beta launch" may come sooner than expected. And after the budget woes and customer service scandals that airlines suffered in 2017, flying the (not-so) friendly skies could get a much-needed upgrade once Jupiter transits into the Archer's realm.

New ways to learn and earn.

Higher education will benefit from Jupiter's college tour of nerdy-cool Sagittarius. From online academies like Udemy and Lynda.com, to new ways snag a degree (without the staggering debt), this transit might reform the way we learn and earn. With globetrotting Jupiter in freedom-loving Sagittarius, we'll find new ways to make a living that don't require us to be chained to a physical location. Think beyond the nine-to-five: Jupiter in entrepreneurial Sagittarius could foster some fascinating startups. Traditional companies may start to encourage "intrapreneurship" (being entrepreneurial within a corporation), offering perks like flexible hours, remote work and other gig-economy benefits that help them retain happy employees. Will the dreaded commute die a merciful death?

This Jupiter cycle can bring new ways to spread a message across the miles. In 1983, Jupiter in Sagittarius brought us the first-ever mobile phones, introduced by Motorola. Jupiter's most recent visit to Sagittarius in 2007 gave us the iPhone, a Sagittarian invention if there ever was one. By November of that year (close to the end of that Jupiter cycle), Apple had sold more than 1.4 million iPhones.

The precursor to the selfie was also born while Jupiter was in Sagittarius. The first Polaroid Land Camera introduced instant photography to the world in 1947. (Interestingly, manufacturing ended in 1983, during a later Jupiter in Sagittarius cycle.) It will be fascinating to see what Jupiter's next spin through Sagittarius will bring, especially since publishing and media also fall under this cosmic umbrella. Will touchscreens and swiping go the way of CD players and cordless phones?

Publishing and broadcasting: A media revolution.

Sagittarius and Jupiter both rule publishing, and indeed the way we consume media has changed. From "fake news" and data-mined "suggestions," from Amazon to the binge-watching and YouTube revolution, anyone can find a platform to air their views. Expansive Jupiter in Sagittarius will bring new developments for consuming and making media. During a 1936 Jupiter transit, the BBC aired its first televised broadcast; forever changing the way news is received. Since Sagittarius rules morals and values, journalistic ethics could become a major topic of debate.

Love thy neighbor: Cross-cultural issues take the stage.

Immigration and cross-cultural issues have become charged topics in the last couple years, and with Jupiter in multicultural Sagittarius, they might

20

"In the best-case scenario, Jupiter in Sagittarius could be a time of cross-cultural harmony and rekindled diplomacy."

take front-burner status. In the best-case scenario, Jupiter in Sagittarius could be a time of cross-cultural harmony and rekindled diplomacy—a welcome relief from the xenophobia that rose while conservative Saturn was in Sagittarius from 2014 to 2017. Orthodox Saturn here brought fearmongering and a rise in hate crimes. Open-minded Jupiter makes us curious about our international neighbors, which can rebuild bridges that were burnt. Immigration policy could get a much-needed makeover, as Jupiter in Sagittarius (which also rules the law) defends freedom of speech and religion.

On the flip side, the doubled vibration of Jupiter in Sagittarius can heap fuel on the fanatical fires, giving rise to political extremism and religious fundamentalism. International politics may get intense. The Immigration Act of 1924 was passed while Jupiter was in Sagittarius, dramatically cutting the number of immigrants allowed into the U.S. That same year, Ellis Island closed as an entry point and became a detention and deportation center for illegal aliens. In 2017, lawyers and judges battled travel bans unfairly targeting Muslims in the United States.

Jupiter in Sagittarius will force us to deal with the lingering divisiveness. We could see major political leaders rise and fall. During past Jupiter in Sagittarius transits, Gandhi and Yitzhak Rabin were murdered, the Dalai Lama fled Tibet and Margaret Thatcher and Fidel Castro took power. The Nixon Watergate scandal also played out while Jupiter was in Sagittarius during the early 1970s.

Worthy causes: Educational reform & ending global poverty.

Looking for a worthy cause while Jupiter is in Sagittarius? Our suggestion: educational reform for girls in developing countries. It's been proven that educating girls and women is the key to eradicating global poverty. One in three girls is married before age 18 in developing nations, and pregnancy complications are the leading cause of death for girls age 15 to 19 worldwide. By contrast, when girls are educated, they can contribute to their economies, breaking the cycle of hunger and poverty. As self-sufficient citizens, they are less likely to contract diseases that ravage their communities and cause widespread deaths.

Yes, that's our soapbox (hey, we're Sagittarians!)—and there will be plenty to preach about while outspoken Jupiter is in the visionary planet's domain. Just watch a tendency to become an "armchair philosopher" with the spotted planet in this lofty, pontificating sign. With Jupiter in truth-teller Sagittarius, people will get fired up to live by their principles. Let's make sure those ideologies are rooted in facts, not false information. ✸

Saturn in Capricorn

Structured Saturn roots into its home sign of Capricorn from December 19, 2017 – December 17, 2020. With potent Pluto also here, deep structural changes are ahead.

Has the patriarchy met its match—or will it grow more deeply entrenched? Structured Saturn, the planetary father figure, is on a three-year tour through its home sign of Capricorn, giving us a double dose of daddy issues. (Note: Saturn will briefly enter Aquarius from March to July 2020, but it won't complete its cycle until that December.) Since Saturn is the astrological ruler of Capricorn, it's most comfortable in this zodiac sign. Can we evolve into the "divine masculine" and use this megadose of male energy for good?

Both Saturn and Capricorn rule men, fathers, authority, banks, the economy, government, corporations and big industry. These are the areas that will come under scrutiny, as Saturn's magnifying glass surveys for flaws in the foundation of leadership and large entities. The global patriarchy could come tumbling down—or press for even more of a takeover.

Saturn returns to Capricorn every 28-30 years, staying for about three years each time. Its imprint on history is indelible, tearing down outmoded structures and revealing some of the worst corruptions among world leadership. Saturn was last in Capricorn from February 13 to June 9, 1988 and then November 11, 1988 to February 6, 1991. As Saturn returns to Capricorn, we must ask ourselves: What are the structures that hold our lives together…and which ones keep us down?

Saturn & Pluto: Both in Capricorn.

With transformational Pluto also in Capricorn from 2008 to 2024, there are seismic shifts going on beneath the surface, sort of like tectonic plates shifting before an earthquake. Pluto rules power and control, secrets and hidden motives. This shadowy planet can expose corruption, or it can alchemize it, raising us to a higher spiritual vibration. Saturn is like an astrological auditor looking for flaws in our structural integrity and even creating breakdowns that force us to fix them for good. In many ways, these planetary players are opposites: Pluto rules the hidden realm, while Saturn governs all that is tangible and concrete. This can also be like a metaphorical volcano rumbling beneath our feet, pushing us to face facts before it explodes.

Will Saturn help shape Pluto's changes into reality or will their joint effort cause more destruction and greed? We may not know fully until January 12, 2020, when these planetary players make an exact meetup. But we'll feel their tremors leading up to

22

it. But here's hoping the end result will be greater clarity and leaders who are truly "for the people."

Saturn and Pluto travel in the same sign every 33 to 38 years. Historically, their union has reshuffled the dynamics of global power. They were conjunct in October 1914, near the outbreak of World War I. In 1948, their close alliance in Leo coincided with Israel's formation and a redistribution of power in the Middle East. The 1982 Saturn-Pluto meetup, in balanced Libra, was a time of economic recession with the highest unemployment rate since the Great Depression (which, incidentally, took place during Saturn's 1929-32 visit to Capricorn).

As Saturn and Pluto make their way through Capricorn, we'll feel their dual impact in government, business and the economy. People will transform the way they work, conduct commerce and deal with hierarchies, perhaps forming their own micro-economies or self-governing communities.

Patriarchy or power to the people?

The past few years, while Saturn was in global Sagittarius, we saw a rise in xenophobia and far-right extremism. Saturn in Capricorn could be a time of harshness, when compassion is in short supply among elected officials. If governments continue to become starker and more authoritarian, people will be compelled to organize en masse, demanding laws and leadership that represent their actual needs.

Saturn's 1988-91 transit through Capricorn brought the Bush Era, along with Operation Desert Storm and the Gulf War. Saturn's return to Capricorn could see more Mideast issues stemming from policies (and global grudges) borne during this last transit.

In the U.S., a largely male government continues to strip and chip away at rights for women, people of color and the poor. Saturn in Capricorn will demand a fight for legislation and policies that protect more than just a privileged elite—but we can also expect great opposition from the Capricorn-ruled "one percenters."

The AstroTwins' 2018 Gemini Planetary Planner

Patriotism and patriarchy could rise with Saturn in the sign of law and order Capricorn. The military and police force may come under further scrutiny. With Pluto here, we'll continue to see corruption exposed in the ranks. But the profiteering might reach new lows as Pluto's tango with big-business Saturn expands the privatized corporate prisons, a.k.a. "the prison industrial complex." While we hope this isn't the case, things may have to get ugly before they improve.

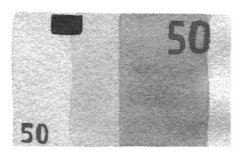

Big business, monopolies & regulations.

On a positive note, Saturn in Capricorn might restore order to our out-of-control world by instituting policies that protect human rights—or by dismantling oppressive laws. Important regulations could be imposed on big businesses that are polluting our planet, causing climate change and melting polar ice caps. Saturn rules harsh lessons and wakeup calls, so here's hoping that it doesn't take anything drastic, especially with intense Pluto at play, to force our hand.

One vision for the interplay of transformational Pluto and Saturn in Capricorn is the birth of a new "eco-economy." We may see a boon for industries like renewable energy (solar and wind) and "geoengineering" products meant to reverse the impact of climate change. Indeed, efforts taken to shrink the hole in the Antarctic ozone layer the last time Saturn was in Capricorn (1988-91) began to show signs of success in 2016. Perhaps "carbon capture" technology will helps us reverse rising global temperatures before it's too late.

Government control and regulation of our food supply could be a huge issue during Saturn in Capricorn. The environmental and health toll of factory farms can no longer be ignored. More and more studies are revealing the downright frightening content in even our so-called healthy manufactured foods, as well as the lack of government inspection of FDA-approved items.

While Saturn was in entrepreneurial Sagittarius from 2014-17, we saw the rise of the gig economy, from Uber and Lyft to Amazon Prime. Saturn and Pluto together in Capricorn could bring stiffer regulations, as well as a few power-mongering monopolies. Interestingly enough, Capricorn Jeff Bezos, the owner of Amazon and the *Washington Post*, engineered a buyout of Whole Foods just before Saturn entered Capricorn. As Amazon begins rolling out retails stores, Bezos may become a poster child for the Saturn-Pluto-Capricorn rise of corporate domination.

Saturn in Capricorn through history: An overview.

To understand what Saturn in Capricorn could bring, it's helpful to review past eras for recurring themes. Saturn's past visits to Capricorn have brought major "people versus the government"

movements. Dictators have risen to power while others came crashing down. Saturn is the great cosmic teacher, and at its best, it can bring impressive leaders who rule with integrity, making historic diplomatic moves.

Powerful leaders protecting the people & environment.

Saturn was in Capricorn in the early 1900s, when U.S. President Teddy Roosevelt, famous for anti-trust laws and "trust-busting," took office. Roosevelt, whose face is carved into Mount Rushmore, was known as "the conservationist president" for his pioneering efforts to protect wildlife and public parks. After creating the United States Forest Service, he established 150 national forests and protected about 230 million acres of public land. As Saturn moves into Capricorn again, these precious lands are in danger of being deregulated and defunded. Here's hoping Roosevelt's legacy rises again—our planet literally depends on it.

Social activism & women's suffrage.

Roosevelt was also a driving force behind the Progressive Movement of the early 20th century, which organized to combat problems created by industrialization, urbanization and government corruption. It was a Saturn in Capricorn crackdown on the waste, greed and excess of the Gilded Age. Corporate trusts, in cahoots with corrupt politicians, were targeted by the Progressive Movement, which pushed for fair wages and the eight-hour workday. Prohibition, which outlawed alcohol, also rose during this conservative Saturn in Capricorn era. Women's suffrage also thrived during this period, as activists gathered and fought for the right to vote. It was a well-timed challenge to the patriarchy, as women demanded to be let into male-only institutions they'd been excluded from. The feminist ideal of the New Woman—a bicycle-riding, educated, independent figure—skyrocketed as Saturn entered Capricorn in the 20th century.

The birth of mass media.

Right as Saturn entered Capricorn in early 1900, the magazine industry boomed. Suppressive Saturn was leaving Sagittarius, the sign of publishing. As Saturn moved into Capricorn, the media and big business buddied up. National magazine advertising soared, allowing publishers to drop the cover price of periodicals to an affordable 10 cents per issue. Along with this came the rise of "muckraking"—journalists tasked with exposing corporate and government corruption, bringing down monopolies, revealing scandals and putting a human face on social ills such as poverty and child labor.

As we move into Saturn in Capricorn again, the mass media is in the spotlight, with journalistic ethics and "fake news" running rampant. The government and journalists are back to being adversarial, with the White House shutting reporters out of standard press briefings. Meanwhile, Google and Facebook algorithms can drive which stories appear in people's social media feeds, undermining credible sources and serving up "alternative facts" masquerading as legitimate news. With Saturn back in Capricorn, mass media is likely to get a much-needed makeover, while the rift between journalism and wealthy power players is likely to grow—which is not necessarily a bad thing.

The Great Depression.

Saturn entered Capricorn in March 1929, briefly backing into Sagittarius from May until November of that year. That summer, the stock market peaked and began declining, due in part to the faltering agricultural economy, excessive bank loans and a proliferation of debt. On October 29, also known as Black Thursday, the stock market crashed. While Saturn returned to Capricorn from November 29, 1929 until February 1932, the Great Depression devastated the U.S. economy. By the time Saturn left this sign, stocks were only worth 20 percent of their 1929 value, nearly half of America's banks had failed and 30 percent of the workforce was unemployed. While we are not predicting a market crash simply because Saturn is returning to Capricorn, certain industries could take a hit, cleaving space for new products and corporate players to emerge.

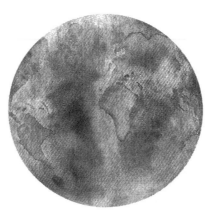

Fidel Castro & the Cold War.

Saturn entered Capricorn on January 5, 1959. Four days prior, Fidel Castro (a Leo) ousted the Capricorn dictator Fulgencio Batista. Soon after, Russia and Cuba got cozy and the Cold War began, leading to a slew of embargos that were recently lifted by Barack Obama. As Saturn was leaving Capricorn in 1961, John F. Kennedy, Jr. came to power and the Bay of Pigs invasion attempted and failed to remove Castro, who went on to become one of the longest ruling heads of state in history.

Gandhi's Passive Resistance movement.

While Saturn toured Capricorn in 1930, Mohandas Gandhi led the Salt March—one of the most famous examples of passive resistance (satyagraha).

For 50 years, salt manufacturing was controlled by a government monopoly. Although salt was easily procured from the sea, it was a crime for Indian citizens to make or get their own salt, because the government charged a tax on it. Gandhi encouraged citizens to refuse this tax by making their own salt or buying it from underground sellers. The 24-day, 240-mile Salt March ended at a beach when Gandhi picked up a handful of salt and held it overhead as a symbol of peaceful protest. This passive resistance movement ultimately led to India's independence from British rule 17 years later.

Stalin's Collectivization: Socialism gone wrong.

In the Soviet Union, an inhumane attempt at government intervention during Saturn's transit through Capricorn led to one of history's worst atrocities. In the early 1930s, Joseph Stalin forced rural farmers to "collectivize" their land, agriculture and livestock, turning over all output to government control. This was touted as a modern miracle: The means of production would be "socialized" and removed from individual control, allowing (ostensibly) for more equal distribution of food. Many farmers protested through acts of sabotage: refusing to produce and harvest crops or even burning theirs. The more successful and

The AstroTwins' 2018 Gemini Planetary Planner   26

"Saturn's past visits to Capricorn have brought major 'people versus the government' movements."

rebellious farmers were shot, deported or put in horrific Gulag labor camps. Collectivism created such huge upheaval around food production that it led to the Soviet famine of 1932-33, which had a death toll of 5 to 10 million Ukrainians. Worse, Stalin withheld huge reserves of grain from the citizens that could have relieved the famine.

Build bridges, not walls: Construction and deconstruction.

Saturn and Capricorn rule constructions and boundaries—including literal walls. The Berlin Wall was built during Saturn's visit to Capricorn in 1961 as a way of stopping Eastern Bloc emigration into Western Europe. This links back to the previous time Saturn was in Capricorn, as people were fleeing Soviet-style regimes created under Stalin's rule. History came full circle when Saturn returned to Capricorn from 1989-91. The Berlin Wall was opened in 1989, and its demolition was underway for the rest of this Saturn transit. As Saturn moves into Capricorn again, Donald Trump continues to press for a U.S.-Mexico border wall.

On a positive note, an architectural renaissance could be in order. Saturn in Capricorn can help us leave impressive (and positive) legacies that stand the test of time. Saturn rules buildings and architecture, and we may see some great new innovations in this arena, especially in the green and sustainable building genre. (Think: solar energy and living roofs for food production in urban areas.) While Saturn was in Capricorn from 1959-61, Frank Lloyd Wright finished the spectacular Guggenheim Museum, his last masterpiece before his death.

Saturn in Capricorn going forward: What have we learned?

How can we prevent troubling history from repeating itself as Saturn returns to Capricorn, placing a double dose of emphasis on systems, governments and authority? We must watch out for oppressive laws and ideologies masquerading as "revolutions." From North Korea's Kim Jong Un (a Capricorn) to Syria's Bashar Al Assad to Venezuela's Nicolas Maduro, we head into the new Saturn in Capricorn cycle with perilous international leadership—and scary examples of patriarchal, authoritarian domination gone awry.

Since Saturn suppresses and Pluto transforms, this era could actually put the kibosh on heavy-handed rulership and patriarchy. "The future is female" was a rallying slogan of 2017's historical Women's March on Washington. As Saturn clamps down on Capricorn's masculine rulership, we may see a rise in female government leaders and women business owners. Statistics show that educating girls and women is one of the vital keys to ending poverty. As women's role in the workforce grows and conscious men help usher in the "divine masculine," gender roles will continue to be reformed. Here's hoping that men and women can work together in service of the planet's survival, uniting around the common cause of our shared humanity. ✳

 The AstroTwins' 2018 Gemini Planetary Planner

Uranus in Taurus

The economy and tradition get an overhaul as Uranus enters Taurus from May 15, 2018 – April 26, 2026.

The more something changes, the more it stays the same? On May 15, Uranus, the planet of revolution, technology and rebellion, moves from firebrand Aries into conservative Taurus. Talk about strange cosmic bedfellows! Unconventional Uranus pushes for radical evolution and progress, while nostalgic Taurus roots in to time-tested traditions, resisting change at every turn.

Uranus only visits each zodiac sign every 84 years, electrifying the airwaves for about seven years and disrupting the status quo. However, Uranus is in its "fall" in Taurus—a weakened position—since the energies are an awkward mismatch.

Uranus in Taurus is a bit like Justin Bieber after age 21, since his self-made success gave way to bad boy behavior. He flaunts all the Uranian trappings: tattoos, fistfights and "outrageous" scandals. But underneath the staged rebellion is a wealthy, privileged mainstream pop star who lives in a mansion and reaps the spoils of patriarchy. One minute he's popping bottles with the Kardashians; the next he's an artsy, brooding outsider deleting his Instagram account.

Uranus focuses on the future while Taurus clings to the past. During this utterly awkward transit, we could all come down with a head-spinning new brand of "Bieber fever," trying to buck the system and benefit from it at the same time.

Taurus' astrological rulership includes money, work, material objects, security, farming, the food supply, the arts and music. All of these areas will be radically revamped as we grapple with this new cosmic conundrum.

Uranus in Aries: A 7-year cycle ends.

Since March 2011, Uranus has been transiting through individualistic, pioneering Aries, igniting radical activism. During this era, we saw the Arab Spring, Occupy Wall Street, the Black Lives Matter movement—plus Marriage Equality and the Women's March. In renegade Aries spirit, the people have raised their voices in the name of inclusion and human rights. On the hotheaded flipside, this cycle also stirred a few frightening fringe uprisings, including violent "alt-right" rallies, ISIS and a spike in post-election hate crimes.

Personal expression skyrocketed with tech-savvy Uranus in solo-star Aries. "Selfie culture" exploded, while anyone with a webcam or a Snapchat handle got a shot at fame. We got YouTube celebrities, viral videos (Chewbacca mom, anyone?) and auto-tuned pop (Rebecca Black's "Friiiday, Friiiday" shall forever ring nasally in our ears). Uranus rules television, which is forever altered. Instead of

28

gathering 'round the family flatscreen for prime-time programs, we now binge-watch on personal devices, making our own TV schedules.

This Uranus cycle also brought some epic indie creations, from Beyonce's "Lemonade" visual album to Netflix's *Orange Is the New Black*. But in capricious Aries style, we forgot that our devices are also sensitive data storage units, putting our identities and personal passcodes at risk. Social media, while an amazing tool for launching independent campaigns and efforts, was used to manipulate the masses with fake news and full-on cyberhacking. Attention spans shortened, Aries style, thanks to our Uranian smartphones, and distracted driver laws had to be put in effect.

Uranus will depart from Aries on May 15, 2018, making one last return here from November 6, 2018 until March 7, 2019. After that, it won't visit Aries again until 2094, so put your personal stamp on the zeitgeist while you can!

Farming & the food supply: Major changes ahead.

Taurus is an earth sign that governs sustenance and self-sufficiency. Farming and the food supply could get a major overhaul. With forward-thinking Uranus here, we may see scientific developments that improve soil quality, help growers and revolutionize the farming industry. Can we pioneer a solution to global hunger—one that doesn't involve factory farms and genetically modified seeds? At this writing, scientists are developing 3D and 4D "printed" food that's actually edible. Microloans and

training programs in rural areas are helping small family farms succeed.

The saying "let food be thy medicine and medicine be thy food" doesn't only apply to your $14 cold-pressed juice anymore. Last year, scientists successfully transformed a spinach leaf into a working human heart muscle. With Uranus in Taurus, we may look to the earth beneath our feet, rather than the latest chemical concoction, to fight diseases.

The end of money? The rise of cashless businesses.

Taurus rules money, and with technological Uranus here, dollars could go digital. Amazon is already testing a new "cashless" technology. Customers enter a brick-and-mortar store with a mobile app that adds items to a virtual cart as they shop. Of course, this has an economic downside, as unskilled human labor will be replaced by robots and algorithms. A New Zealand company called Soul Machines is already marketing its

"The saying 'let food be thy medicine and medicine be thy food' doesn't just apply to your $14 cold-pressed juice anymore."

Digital Humans—robots imbued with "emotional intelligence" that can replace living, breathing customer service assistants. You probably won't miss the shopgirl who follows you to the dressing room and coos about how "adorable" an ill-fitting item looks. But the alternative is a little sci-fi freaky, too.

As A.I. replaces human labor, our relationship with money could go through a massive shift. Out of necessity, people may adopt the barter system, or take up the "gift economy" that's practiced at festivals like Burning Man. In this model, no cash changes hands, and goods or services are offered from a spirit of generosity. Wanna start a commune, anyone?

Economic makeovers afoot.

Taurus rules the economy, and the term "Bull Market" is about to get a Uranian makeover. Brexit could be a prelude to shakeups of Wall Street and banking. Interestingly, the Boston Tea Party took place during a previous Uranus in Taurus cycle, when demonstrators protested "taxation without representation." And the U.S. spent the entire last Uranus in Taurus transit climbing out of the Great Depression, which ended in 1941, right as Uranus departed from Taurus. President Roosevelt also signed the U.S. Social Security act, providing unemployment compensation and pensions for the elderly. This go-round, Medicaid and affordable health care are up for Uranus-style reform.

From selfies to self-sufficiency: Using technology for practical gain.

Death to the cubicle? With indie-spirited Uranus in hardworking Taurus, the gig economy will grow even bigger. More people will work remotely and in co-working spaces, and the full-time employment model will continue to go the way of the dinosaurs.

Uranus in sensible, profit-driven Taurus can help us monetize our creations in interesting new ways.

Sensible Taurus could change the type of businesses that get funded. Rather than sink a load of venture capital into yet another social-sharing app, startup support may go to practical inventions that improve our daily lives. For better or worse, data mining will continue, as businesses are pushed to meet customer demands and habits.

The rise of populism and dictatorship.

The worst manifestations of Uranus in Taurus can be bigotry, stubbornness and warmongering. Adolf Hitler, a Taurus, seized power just as Uranus was ending its last transit of Aries, and retained his

2018 HIGHLIGHTS

"Uranus in sensory Taurus will alter the way we interact with the physical and digital worlds."

dictatorial grip through the 1930s, while Uranus was in Taurus. Mussolini also came into power during this last Uranus in Taurus transit, spreading fascism. As we enter the same cycle 84 years later, extreme right-wing candidates are once again on the rise, spinning propaganda through social media, slanted news outlets, populist rallies and cyber hacking. In the past few years, Uranus in Aries has provoked violent disruptors, many using technology to plot public acts of terrorism or to spread messages of hate. Hopefully, we will learn from history and not underestimate the "fringe" groups' ability to organize and gain critical mass.

Living in a post-material world?

Taurus rules the physical world and material objects. With freedom-seeking Uranus in sensual Taurus, we'll want to enjoy our possessions without being chained to them. But we'll also want to own, rather than rent, as financially-savvy Taurus invests for the long haul.

The past Uranus in Aries cycle brought us opportunities to unshackle ourselves from the

9-to-5 lifestyle, with solo venture options such as Airbnb, Lyft, and co-op office spaces like WeWork gaining massive popularity. But there are also drawbacks, such as a lack of benefits and no return on investment. Now, people may trend more toward owning a "share" of these places, perhaps receiving stock options in a company where they are independent contractors, or building equity instead of just getting a check.

From virtual reality to mixed reality.

Think your virtual reality goggles are all that? Uranus in sensory Taurus will alter the way we interact with the physical and digital worlds. The VR world is developing ways to include smell, touch and taste from afar. Inventor Adrian David Cheok is spearheading the Mixed Reality Lab, which will engage all five senses in a simulated experience. Email us a cheeseburger, would ya, Dave?

This Uranus phase could also take the IoT ("internet of things") beyond the "smart" house or driverless

> "Time for some protest anthems—and new ways to get #woke? With Uranus in Taurus, ruler of the voice and throat, folk songs could make a next-generation comeback."

car. Perhaps we'll trade swiping and scrolling for computerless computing, as our digital devices become one with everyday household objects.

Arts & music: A digital revolution.

Time for some protest anthems—and new ways to get #woke? With Uranus in Taurus, ruler of the voice and throat, folk songs could make a next-generation comeback. Fine art, literature and dance will meet community activism and digital media (Uranus' domain), giving rise to stunning and stirring creations.

Prior to the airwaves and Internet being primary sources for breaking from tradition and questioning authority, Walt Whitman published his infamous and, at the time, shocking, "Leaves of Grass" in 1855 while Uranus was in Taurus. It was an ode to nature, earthly pleasure, and sensual love—going so far as to ponder life and death in novel ways.

During the 1934 Uranus in Taurus transit, ex-pat author Gertrude Stein returned to the United States for a lecture tour. She resided unapologetically in Paris with her lover, Alice B. Toklas, holding salons for their numerous and varied literary and activist friends. That same year, Taurus and surrealist painter Salvador Dali's works were introduced to the United States, becoming an instant sensation.

However, his apolitical public stance (he refused to publicly denounce Hitler and fascism) and public stunts got him in so much trouble that his peers subjected him to a "trial." All of these individuals were well ahead of their times. We look forward to seeing what kind of visionaries Uranus in Taurus reveals this time around.

The space race heats up.

Earth to Taurus, do you copy? Uranus rules space travel, and interestingly, the Mars One Project was founded just as Uranus entered Aries, which is ruled by Mars. With Uranus in Taurus, we may find our inner Matt Damon and start the first attempts to build and farm in space. Who knows? In 2026, Mars moves into Gemini, the ruler of neighborhoods and transportation. Maybe we'll pave the way for Earth's first interplanetary settlers. ✳

2018

YOUR YEAR AHEAD
Sun Sign Horoscope

Gemini 2018

GEMINI MAY 21-JUNE 20

The Highlights

LOVE

The good news: Tough Saturn has ended a three-year trek through your opposite sign of Sagittarius, a challenging cycle that put your partnerships to the test. And in November, lucky Jupiter arrives, attracting exciting growth and long-term prospects. But your work's not done: Saturn is now in your eighth house of intimacy, teaching your tough but crucial lessons about how relationships are built to last. Prepare to face any fears and trust issues, clearing the path for happily-ever-after through hard work and humility.

MONEY & CAREER

New work opportunities arise this year, as enterprising Jupiter visits your diligent sixth house. You're learning to delegate, organize and run life like a well-oiled machine. Bored or between gigs? You might just take an interim "bridge job" to pay the bills while you figure out your next moves. July's eclipse in your money house could bring an exciting opportunity—a good reason not to rush into anything too permanent! With studious Saturn in your long-term wealth zone, it's time to learn more about investing, real

estate and passive income. You could get serious about paying off debt and building a nest egg.

HEALTH & WELLNESS

Lunges, squats and Burpees, oh my! Expansive Jupiter is in your sixth house of health and fitness, pushing you to make wellness an adventure. Clean eating and plenty of movement are the stars' prescription for happiness—and all the better if you can run around outdoors! Fresh air and nature will reset you, and with innovative Uranus starting an eight-year visit to your holistic and mystical twelfth house this May, contemplative time near water can soothe your soul.

FAMILY & FRIENDS

Sift through your inner circle—and tighten the borders a bit. Stern Saturn and shadowy Pluto in your intimate eighth house reveals the leakers and haters in your midst. Have you been too quick to trust? A few loyalty tests wouldn't hurt, Gemini. Fascinating new friends could pop up, both locally and from afar, thanks to four of this year's eclipses that draw inspiring kindred spirits your way. ✸

   The AstroTwins' 2018 Gemini Planetary Planner

2018 ASTROLOGY OVERVIEW

GEMINI Horoscope

Power Dates for Gemini

GEMINI NEW MOON
June 13

GEMINI FULL MOON
November 23

GEMINI SOLAR RETURN
May 20–June 21

Steady as she goes! In 2018, the astrological emphasis is on stability. That's not a concept that Geminis normally gravitate toward, but it's one you may welcome with open arms now. Until November, expansive Jupiter is visiting Scorpio and your sixth house of health, daily work and organization. Suddenly, you want order in the Gemini court! And who could blame you? Jupiter spent a good part of last year in Libra and your dramatic fifth house, bringing excitement but a fair share of chaos or upheaval. Now, it's time to simplify and prioritize. Less is more!

Hard work and steady progress will pay off now, both at the office and in your life. You're inspired to create systems that keep life humming along, and to treat your body like a temple. Get into the groove of daily work and routines, enjoying that pleasant vibe of being "in the zone."

It doesn't matter so much what you're doing as it does how you feel while you're doing it. And your diligence will certainly pay off, perhaps near the July 12 Cancer solar eclipse, which could bring a new work or moneymaking opportunity out of the blue.

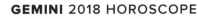
Adventurous Jupiter in your wellness zone makes this the perfect year for clean eating, regular exercise and time enjoying nature. Fresh air and fitness: your prescription for happiness in 2018. Some Geminis may get doctor's orders to move more, or a health issue may require you to tune into your body instead of ignoring it. This could be a blessing in disguise, especially if it forces you to slow down and dial back excessive stress. Gemini, your sign isn't famous for knowing your limits (what are those, anyway?), but too much multitasking will wear you out. Aim to balance mind, body and spiritual pursuits and live a more balanced life.

You'll be celestially spurred onward—and inward—right before your birthday. On May 15, changemaker Uranus makes a huge leap, entering Taurus and your twelfth house of closure, healing and spirituality for the first time in 77 years. With this pioneering planet here, you could become deeply involved in metaphysics, energy work or holistic wellness. You might begin a path of recovery from an addiction or begin the kind of eye-opening inner work that leads you to make sweeping lifestyle changes. Uranus will be here until April 2026, provoking a deep, soul-level makeover. Since this progress-driven planet rules technology, you might connect with a spiritual community online or sell your own healing services virtually.

Toward the end of the year, exciting partnership opportunities could arise. On November 8, wholehearted Jupiter will enter your opposite sign of Sagittarius for 13 months, drawing inspiring people into your orbit. Get ready for a relationship revolution, or some dynamic business duos. Longtime couples or work partners could evolve,

moving into new roles or seeking adventurous horizons to tackle together. A lucrative overseas client could come your way, or you may start traveling to explore a joint work venture. Single Geminis could meet someone with life-partner potential, and—surprise!—they may be nothing like the person you envisioned yourself walking the aisle with. You could connect with someone of a wildly different background or even fall into a long-distance love affair. Will relocation be in the stars? You'll need until 2019 to figure that part out. For now, explore with an open heart and mind.

And before you rush into anything permanent, sober Saturn puts some yellow caution tape around eager Jupiter's starry-eyed plans. Saturn is now in Capricorn until 2020, putting weight on your eighth house of intimacy, joint ventures and mergers. Rather than rush to put a ring on it, obey the ringed taskmaster and take it slow. Or slow-ish…Jupiter's tantalizing powers can only be resisted so much! Just make sure that any alliances you get into can go the distance. Now is the time for partnerships that are exciting but also built to last.

Jupiter in Scorpio: Healthy choices.
October 10, 2017–November 8, 2018

Healthy, wealthy and wise? This trinity could be your recipe for success this year, Gemini, as bountiful Jupiter lunges and squats its way through Scorpio and your orderly, fitness-focused sixth house. After an indulgent and dramatic 2017, you're ready to streamline and simplify.

Last year's focus was on love, creativity and relationships. You wore your heart on your sleeve

> ## "With expansive Jupiter in your wellbeing zone, health becomes a priority. You might get serious about clean eating, regular exercise and a toxin-free lifestyle."

and let emotions guide you. In some ways, this was good for your heady sign. Contrary to your "wild and crazy" reputation, many Geminis actually have a controlling side, especially when it comes to their feelings. But with outspoken Jupiter here, the floodgates broke open. A romance or creative project may have consumed your time, which left the rest of your life in a bit of disarray.

Now, your analytical side takes the wheel, and your focus turns to practical matters. You want systems and processes that make life run like a well-oiled machine. Call in the cleanup crews and book the personal trainer! Unfurl your Feng Shui bagua map and declutter your money corner—or go full Marie Kondo and get rid of things that "don't inspire joy." Less is more!

This cycle, which only happens every 12 years, may not be the "sexiest" time of your life, but it will certainly be grounding. Philosophical Jupiter helps you find the adventure in the little things—which is actually a beautiful way to be. While you might find yourself sweating the small stuff (there will be a lot of it!), you'll also appreciate the little things and enjoy life's simpler pleasures. Jupiter was last in Scorpio from October 25, 2005 until November 23, 2006. Look back to that time, if you can remember it, for clues of what could resurface.

With expansive Jupiter in your wellbeing zone, health becomes a priority. You might get serious

about clean eating, regular exercise and a toxin-free lifestyle. Turn self-care into an adventure,: try upbeat group classes (such as a dance-yoga-cardio fusion) or combine physical activity with time in nature. The great outdoors will revive your soul, whether you're biking, gardening or doing Burpees on the beach. A pet could bring joy this year.

Caveat: Jupiter is the god of the feast, so even if you're eating healthy fare, your appetite (and by association, your waistline) can expand during this indulgent Jupiter cycle. You may go up a size or two but have perfect health in your checkups—and if so, you might just embrace the new curves or cushioning. Or, use this opportunity to dive into curious Jupiter's love of learning, and research nutrition and healthy living. Which foods agree with your systems? Do you need more vitamins or supplements? Get a full panel of tests done. The sixth house rules the digestive system, and you may benefit from taking a daily probiotic, trying colon hydrotherapy or improving your "gut health." Swap chemical-laden cleaning and beauty products for natural ones. If eating organic seems too pricey, you could join a CSA (community-supported agriculture) co-op that gives an affordable weekly bundle of local produce.

For some Geminis, Jupiter in the sixth house can reveal a health diagnosis or bring doctor's orders to make a lifestyle change. This could be a blessing in disguise, especially if it leads to early detection.

Stress has been linked to many diseases, so even the fittest of Geminis should make a dedicated effort to reduce it. If you have a sedentary job, get up and move every hour or try out a standing desk. Keep that inner micromanager in check—just because you can do ten people's jobs, doesn't mean you should. Recommended reading for Type A Geminis: *The Big Leap* by Gay Hendricks, which distinguishes between your Zone of Excellence (things you're good at but not passionate about) and your Zone of Genius (things you're naturally gifted at and love to do). Inch your way into the genius zone this year.

The sixth house also governs your work processes. How organized are you and where could you have better systems that will keep your life humming along efficiently? There's a Type A side to every Gemini—you're ruled by intellectual Mercury, after all—and this year, it can come out with a vengeance. Prepare to give the other Mercury-ruled sign, Virgo, a run for its micromanaging money! From spreadsheets to budgeting apps to hiring a virtual assistant, you'll be on a mission to keep life feeling sane and simplified, even as you grow.

The sixth house rules helpful people, and you'll do well learning how to delegate to capable assistants and specialists. Time is money, Gemini—you don't have to do it all yourself! The hours you'll save could be used to hone your craft or take better care of your body. Just be kind to the people you train or pass the torch to, taking the time to explain your process. You might put together an instruction manual that breaks it down step-by-step. That way, you have a better chance of them doing everything to your exacting standards!

Feeling bored with your job? Hunting for a new gig? Don't rush into anything permanent if you're not sure what you want. This year is better spent sharpening your tools than suffering in something that's the wrong fit. With free-spirited Jupiter in your administrative sixth house, this year could be perfect for a "bridge job"—something easy and breezy that doesn't drain your vital energy.

Save your brain cells and energy for productive learning in your off hours. Jupiter rules higher education, making this an ideal transit to polish your skills, earn certifications, or work toward mastery. If you have to do "practice" sessions to get really good at your craft, or work a set number of unpaid hours to earn a state license, this would be the ideal time to do it. The barter system can pay off—for example, you could build your entrepreneurial friend a free website as a way of learning Wordpress design, or you might apprentice with a craftsperson to get an inside glimpse of their expertise. Sitting at the feet of a master is worth every unpaid internship hour during this Jupiter transit, which favors experience-based learning.

A job offer could arrive from the service industry or a "green" sector, or you might be drawn to explore booming areas in wellness and technology. Some of the least sexy-sounding jobs are the most stable now, so you might be inspired to explore fields such as solar power, occupational therapy or computer coding. During this Jupiter transit, your top goal might be to earn a steady paycheck in a field you enjoy, where you'll always be gainfully employed. With outspoken Jupiter in this nature-loving zone, you could become an advocate for climate change prevention or wildlife preservation.

 The AstroTwins' 2018 Gemini Planetary Planner

Creative work, perhaps for a world-bettering cause, could be part of this year's cosmic lineup. From May through August, Jupiter will travel in a rare and harmonious trine (120-degree angle) to healing Neptune, which is in Pisces and your tenth house of success. You'll go farther by adopting an attitude of humble service, rather than trying to elbow your way to the top or "make" things happen. Cutting corners and forcing an agenda will flop, especially with Jupiter in your meticulous sixth house.

Karmic Neptune is a pro at manifesting, so engage in creative visualization as part of your search for a higher calling. During this Jupiter-Neptuen mashup, you're called to deeply examine your motives: Why do you want something so badly? Is the payoff for you and you alone, or will it benefit the world at large? Greed won't be rewarded during this Jupiter-Neptune alignment, but loyal leadership will. As your fellow Gemini John F. Kennedy, Jr. famously said in his Inaugural address, "Ask not what your country can do for you, but what you can do for your country." Apply this to your ambitious pursuits, and you'll rise to rewarding heights.

Jupiter in Sagittarius: Partner up!

November 8, 2018–December 2, 2019

Table for two, please! In November, Jupiter will sail into Sagittarius and your partnership house, blessing you with a 13-month cycle of major relationship growth. Talk about balm for your soul! As the zodiac's Twin, your sign is happiest when you have an adventurous plus-one by your side! And you'll have plenty of options as 2018 draws to a close. Jupiter could bring a bounty of compatible people into your sphere, from a long-term romantic partner to an inspiring business collaborator.

Worldly Jupiter could spark synergy with someone from another culture or background, perhaps a person you meet while traveling. A long-distance romance could heat up, or you could launch an entrepreneurial project with someone in another zip code. Risk-taker Jupiter inspires you to roll the dice: nothing ventured, nothing gained!

Your existing commitments will also go through changes, as you adjust the levels of give-and-take to create more harmony and equality. Longtime couples could renew their vows, travel together or shift into different roles. For example, if you've been the breadwinner, your mate could suddenly become the household high earner. If you're always the star, prepare to play Best Supporting Actor.

Has a relationship run its course? If you've outgrown your connection, philosophical Jupiter could find you parting ways amicably. Don't plan on being single for long, though! Jupiter in Sagittarius could call in a serious contender who balances you out beautifully. Caveat: You'll need to stretch beyond your comfort zone and relinquish a little control. But with adventurous Jupiter steering the ship, you'll quickly see the benefits of trading your tight grip for inspiring companionship.

Saturn in Capricorn: Intimate ties.

December 19, 2017–December 17, 2020

Let's be honest: "forever" isn't a word that your changeable sign takes to readily. Well, Gemini, the next three years have some interesting lessons in store about intimacy, merging and permanent commitments—the kind that you can't back out of on a whim.

Serious Saturn, the planet of maturity, structure

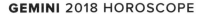

and integrity, has shifted into Capricorn and your eighth house of permabonding. It's time to get serious about your relationships and to strengthen any shaky areas. Saturn rewards hard work and dedication, and it cracks the whip when we try to cut corners. Call in the experts and mentors, from financial advisors to couple's therapists. Saturn's tests often demand professional guidance. You can't life-hack or DIY your way through every situation, and with Saturn here, there's no faking it 'til you make it.

The eighth house rules shared finances and property, which will add heft to your long-term wealth planning. Saturn gets you serious about stuff like consolidating debt, buying or selling real estate or paying off back taxes. Merging your money should not be done lightly, so before you leap into any joint ventures, research the heck out of the other party. Pay an attorney to review or draft contracts and protect your intellectual assets. If you're engaged, this might be the time for a pre-nup, or at least, to keep some things in your own name.

When it comes to money, set your sights on slow and steady growth. Don't expect overnight results for anything you do. Slowly but surely, you could start earning passive income or returns on investments, as long as you stay the course. While you should avoid get-rich-quick ideas and pyramid schemes like the plague, you might explore legitimate affiliate opportunities, such as an Amazon store or reselling an online program you love for commission. If there's a product that's changed your life—an essential oil or supplement, for example—you might become a distributor through a direct sales program. Be discerning and research thoroughly.

Obviously you'll want to keep this as a side hustle instead of quitting your day job. Think of this as a little extra padding, not income you rely on—at least, for now.

Some Geminis will move into binding arrangements: cohabitation, marriage, starting a family, opening a shared business. Don't rush, though! Saturn in your eighth house is like a long engagement—a chance to work out the kinks and discover any obstacles that could interfere with a relationship's longevity. You'll find out exactly how "ready" you are for the big leagues, because Saturn will test your mettle. Like a building inspector searching for flaws in the foundation, Saturn demands that everything is up to code before the ribbon-cutting ceremony. If you discover that you're not quite there, don't force yourself to move forward. You don't have to call off the wedding (literally or metaphorically), but postponing might be the best idea. Saturn's lessons can be inconvenient and deeply humbling—but in the long run, they can save you loads of heartache!

Libido: missing in action? Repressive Saturn in your erotic eighth house can dim your mojo for a minute. You could be consumed with weighty emotions or processing some heavy baggage, which doesn't exactly put you in a frisky mood. Maybe the permanence of a commitment has put a damper on the fantasy that first turned you on. Where's the mystery, the longing? Seeing the same person day in, day out—with sweatpants, breakouts and morning breath—isn't really doing it for you.

What's a playful and lusty Gemini to do? During this transit, you may resonate with the teachings of psychotherapist Esther Perel, a modern love author

 The AstroTwins' 2018 Gemini Planetary Planner

and TED speaker who explores the tension between humans' dueling needs for security and novelty. Perel, a psychotherapist, explores how autonomy can keep relationships feeling alive. Her books *Mating in Captivity: Unlocking Erotic Intelligence* and *The State of Affairs: Rethinking Infidelity* can provide grounding perspective during any turbulent times.

Get a doctor's opinion before you head to divorce court, Gemini. Your hormone levels can greatly influence your sexual desire—and the only "chemistry" that's off could be your biochemistry. You might check out programs such as the Flo Living Center (www.floliving.com), which helps clients with fertility and hormone stabilization through changes in diet, exercise and nutrition. For women, this Saturn phase could bring changes to your cycle and reproductive system. If you're trying to get pregnant, Saturn could make it a bit more challenging.

Single Geminis, take it easy on yourself. You could feel daunted by the idea of putting yourself out there with cautious Saturn at the helm. Trust issues and past-based anxieties could arise. Don't force yourself into halfhearted Tinder-ing. Your time could be better used working with a therapist or healer to get to the heart of these fears. Through diligence, and by facing your shadow, you'll emerge stronger and more self-aware—truly ready for the level of vulnerability that an intimate relationship demands.

Saturn was last in Capricorn from 1988 to 1991, so if you're old enough to remember that time, you may find patterns repeating themselves. This go-round, Saturn will be joining transformational

Pluto, which is in Capricorn from 2008 until 2024. This could be an interesting combo because Pluto rules the hidden aspects of ourselves, while Saturn gives everything tangible form. Deep emotions that have been secretly brewing could break the surface in 2018.

Mystical Pluto and grounded Saturn in this esoteric realm hone your healing gifts and boost your interest in spirituality. Your own psychic abilities could sharpen. You might explore practitioners who specialize in Reiki, acupuncture, past-life regression or hypnotherapy. If you've been struggling with addiction or mental health issues, the combined influence of Saturn and Pluto will make those impossible to ignore. There's no shame in reaching out for support—we can't fix our problems alone, Gemini.

Are the people on Team Gemini worthy of inner-circle status? Untrustworthy operators will be exposed by Saturn and Pluto, and you'll no longer be able to look the other way when their shady behavior arises. Geminis are excellent storytellers, but the danger of this is that you can deceive yourself, or only see the parts of people that serve your narrative. This year's stars will open your eyes, forcing you to face the whole truth.

The best insurance policy: Surround yourself with friends who operate from the highest place of integrity. On that note, are you doing the same? This cycle can attract people who mirror parts of yourself that need to heal and evolve. Before you point the finger of blame, take inventory of your own behavior. Is there deflection or projection going on? We're not saying you should stick around

42

in a draining or abusive situation. But reclaim your power by owning your choices and making better ones going forward.

Uranus in Taurus: Going deep.

May 15, 2018–April 26, 2026

Who are the people you call friends? That cast of characters has changed dramatically in the past seven years. While you still may have your true-blue crew, you've connected with some cutting-edge collaborators and joined a new soul tribe or two.

This is the handiwork of revolutionary Uranus, which entered Aries and your eleventh house of groups back in March 2011, shaking up the status quo. With Uranus in this radical and technology-driven zone, some Gems became quite a presence on social media—for better or worse. (Geminis Kanye West and Donald Trump both sowed their share of Uranian chaos and controversy with Twitter rants during this cycle.) In group scenarios, you've been the person willing to rock the boat or take an unorthodox path. You've gained new followers and alienated others. With Uranus in this political zone, you may have become a spokesperson for an important social cause.

Uranus only visits each sign every 84 years, and this May 15, the side-spinning planet will move into Taurus, activating your twelfth house of healing, closure and the subconscious until 2026. Life could get a little trippy! Uranus will plunge you into more internal waters, a rich time for spiritual and creative development. You've been a fixture on certain social scenes, but Uranus in Taurus sparks a desire for solitude and retreat.

Turn inward, Gemini. Your best work will now be done behind the scenes. This could be a powerful time for recovery from an addiction, deep forgiveness work or healing codependence. Trailblazing Uranus helps you summon the courage to plumb your own emotional depths and face the unknown. Therapy and spiritual counseling can be especially powerful, but beware falling under the spell of a guru figure. With Uranus in this passive zone, you're tempted to hand your authority over to a charismatic person. Remember, someone can guide you to finding answers, but they already exist within you.

Mirror, mirror: The next seven years will give you a front-row seat to the parts of yourself that need healing or evolving. The twelfth house rules aspects that we disown or project onto others. Shame, past trauma, insecurity—all of the "demons"— could make an appearance as Uranus exposes your shadow side. How will you know? A person will enter your life who irritates you, pushes your buttons or seems bent on sabotaging your success. You'll encounter scenarios where control eludes your grasp or you're caught embarrassingly off-guard.

When this happens, don't fight—surrender. Recognize that you're being shown crucial information about yourself. This person or situation is simply reflecting something that's happening within you. And you're either in denial about it or it's a "blind spot" that you need to investigate. As the saying goes, you've got to deal in order to heal.

Avoid falling into a victim mindset. If you find yourself thinking, "Why is this happening to me?" look inward first. Ask yourself, where does this situation reveal where I may not be operating with integrity?

Uranus can be jarring when it delivers a wakeup call. But its sole intention is to incite change and progress. If you've been ignoring a nagging physical or mental health issue, get it checked out. With Uranus in this health-conscious zone, symptoms that flare are a blessing in disguise, helping you detect a problem before it gets any bigger.

With shock-jock Uranus in this mystical zone until 2026, you could undergo a spiritual and emotional makeover. You may receive undeniable "signs" that awaken your higher consciousness: repeating number sequences (such as glancing at the clock and seeing 11:11 or 4:44), déjà vu moments, vivid dreams that are prophetic or involve a departed loved one. Your views on life and death may change, and you may develop psychic abilities. Your beliefs could undergo a radical transformation.

The twelfth house rules institutions and parts of society that are hidden away, including hospitals, jails and impoverished communities. You may become passionate about an issue related to this: reform of the prison system or cutting-edge health treatments and clinical trials. Maybe you'll lead retreats, visit an ashram or spend time at an artist's colony. Going off the grid can lead to major epiphanies about life and your soul purpose.

Uranus will be retrograde from August 7, 2018 until January 6, 2019. It will dip back into Aries for one final hurrah on November 6, giving you one last chance to clean up your social circles and

boost your online presence. Uranus will hunker into Taurus for the long haul on March 7, 2019 and it will stay until April 26, 2026. After that it will move into Gemini, which will bring an exciting seven-year cycle of reinvention. Until then, think of yourself as being on a spiritual and emotional decluttering mission, stripping away what no longer serves you, to make room for a bold new chapter.

Eclipses in Leo & Aquarius: Say what?

January 31, February 15, July 27, August 11

Say what? You're a consummate communicator, Gemini, and this year's game-changing eclipses could give your verbal and intellectual gifts a few chances to shine. Four of 2018's five eclipses will fall on the Leo/Aquarius axis, igniting your third house of local action, ideas and self-expression (ruled by Leo) and your ninth house of travel, study and entrepreneurship (powered by Aquarius).

These eclipses, which will span from February 2017 until January 2019, are here to reshape the way you think, speak and present yourself. You could gain recognition as a thought leader or an influencer on social media. Is there a book or a blog in you, waiting to hatch? Your message, no matter what the medium, could have far-reaching influence in 2018. Opportunities to build your platform—or just spontaneously step up to the mic—could come when you least expect them. Be ready to pitch at a moment's notice!

The saying "think globally, act locally" could become your mantra in 2018, as the eclipses push you to take a more vocal role in your community.

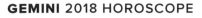

"The saying 'think globally, act locally' could become your mantra in 2018, as the eclipses push you to take a more vocal role in your community. Maybe you get involved in homegrown activism or become a voice of change in your neighborhood."

Maybe you get involved in homegrown activism or become a voice of change in your neighborhood. Teaming up with like-minded people around a shared agenda can take your plans to new heights. Keep an eye out for kindred spirits, both in-person and virtually. Siblings, neighbors and colleagues could play an important role.

While you're busy becoming a local sensation, cross-cultural and international synergies can also heat up. You could be tapped as a motivational speaker or see your work published. This could be one of those years that you become "really big in Asia" or find success in surprising places off the beaten path.

Cancer Solar Eclipse: Money magic.

July 12

Money momentum: Incoming! On July 12, a partial solar (new moon) eclipse arrives in Cancer, rippling through your work and finance sector. Eclipses bring unexpected news designed to wake us up and inspire big shifts. This could plant the seeds for a raise, promotion or an entirely new gig. It's the very first in a series of eclipses on the Cancer/Capricorn axis, which will reform your approach to spending, saving and investing between now and July 2020.

Over the next two years, you could buy or sell property, earn passive income and get savvier about your nest egg. This first eclipse, the only one from this grouping in 2018, prompts you to prepare. Start by getting all your ducks (and ducats) in a row. If you're the type who never even looks at your bank balance, make it a weekly practice. Our friend Kate Northrup, author of *Money: A Love Story*—which you should totally put on your summer reading list—recommends checking it daily, even if it's negative. And if you've got a li'l nest egg going, look into ways you can multiply it.

This eclipse also helps you start a new habit or routine. If you're, say, thinking of going vegan, this can be a good time to begin the process. The results of this eclipse will unfold in the next six months. You'll also get a complimentary confidence boost, since the second house rules self-worth. ✶

GEMINI: HOTSPOTS **BY MONTH**

January: Love Hotspots

January 9: Venus-Pluto meetup

Love planet Venus aligns with the transformational dwarf planet in your intimate eighth house, sparking some soulful confessions. Spoken with compassion, the truth can set you free—and deepen your bond. Sizzling but unspoken chemistry could ignite, possibly with someone a little taboo. Are they checking you out…or is it just your imagination? Under this surreptitious alignment, you can't be certain, but you seem to be picking up signals. You could meet someone and feel a deep déjà-vu.

January 11-31: Mercury in Capricorn

With communicative Mercury in your intimate eighth house for the rest of the month, you could finally have that soul-baring talk, discuss plans for the future or make things more official. Solid couples may be inspired to look at real estate listings or combine funds into a joint account.

January 12: Mercury-Saturn meetup

The communication planet aligned with serious Saturn creates the perfect setting to share your feelings—and perhaps a secret or fantasy you've been keeping to yourself. Honesty is a good policy, but to keep a little intrigue alive, don't feel the need to tell everything. Make sure people have earned your trust first.

January 13: Venus-Uranus square

You want what you want when you want it (#GeminiProblems). But seeking instant gratification could lead you to pursue an attraction that isn't ultimately healthy. Dating online? Take things slow with a virtual connection, even if you chat well into the night and feel an instant click. Apply the same caution if you feel sparks with a friend. Once you go there, it's not so easy to undo.

January 16: Capricorn new moon

This is the beginning of a deep six-month cycle emphasizing intimacy, sex and permanent bonding. It's a good time for singles to plant the seeds for merging or, if you're attached, to make a fresh start around trust and connection.

January 17-February 10: Venus in Aquarius

Freedom's just another word for…aphrodisiac? What you're craving more than anything is independence. Stay open to new options, like pursuing a cross-cultural attraction or booking spontaneous travel, especially with the likelihood of some hot romancing!

January 24: Mercury-Pluto meetup

When the communication planet colludes with penetrating Pluto, it might spark some true confessions. Be careful who you share with: This is a super intense day for bonding through open and honest talk, but not everyone has earned that level of trust.

January 26-March 17: Mars in Sagittarius

The passionate planet kicks off an electrifying tour of your partnership house for the next two months. Couples can bring sexy back to your bond. Start by

resolving not to fight all week. If you can pull it off, you'll enjoy each other's company more than you have in a while. Single? Things could get hot—and official—fast!

January: Career Hotspots

January 1: Cancer full moon (supermoon)
The year starts with a "money moment," as this fiscally-minded full moon reveals steps you can take to increase your earnings and grow a nest egg. Set intentions for where you'd like to be when the July 12 Cancer solar eclipse will reveal your next major moves.

January 6: Mercury-Uranus trine
Sometimes "hive mind" produces more and better ideas than toiling on your own. You'll enjoy working with others today and could land on a brilliant idea.

January 6: Mars-Jupiter meetup
You're in the mood to dream big today, so avoid the nitty-gritty detail work—it could leave you seriously stressed out. Find a way to take care of your basic duties while saving plenty of time for the all-important visioning. And whatever happens, be careful not to bite off more than you can chew.

January 9: Sun-Pluto meetup
When these two heavyweights align in your intensely focused eighth house, you'll feel your own power surge. Don't dim the light on your strategic abilities. Those masterful moves could lead the troops to victory today.

January 11-31: Mercury in Capricorn
Mental Mercury spends the rest of the month in your eighth house of wealth and financial planning. It's a good time to discuss money and joint ventures or to renegotiate shared initiatives. Keep your focus long-term, reviewing your projections to make sure your investments and savings are on the right strategic track.

January 16: Capricorn new moon
The year's only new moon in grounded Capricorn and your investment corner can help you plant the seeds for long-range security. Talk to a financial adviser about how you can (safely) be a bit more aggressive with your investments. An opportunity that involves passive income, real estate or a joint venture could develop over the next six months.

January 24: Mercury-Pluto meetup
Hold a power summit or strategy session today, keeping things ultra-confidential. Be careful about signing anything binding without doing a ton of research first. It's a great day for joining forces with a power player.

January 26-March 17: Mars in Sagittarius
Partnerships can heat up and move quickly into official status over the next two months. You could feel energized by a creative cohort but also a little stressed out when they make "demands" instead of suggestions. Let them know how you feel before resentment builds. Don't rush into binding contracts, even if you're pumped to partner up. Take your time to conduct due diligence so you can move forward without any unanswered questions.

 The AstroTwins' 2018 Gemini Planetary Planner

January 28: Mercury-Uranus square

Don't share your trade secrets with just anyone, as people could be flaky or fickle—or worse, steal your best ideas. This might be the perfect moment to get them to sign a confidentiality agreement. Everywhere in your life, protect sensitive data and update your passwords.

January 31-February 17: Mercury in Aquarius

When the quicksilver planet beams into your expansive and adventurous ninth house, you won't need encouragement to think outside the box or take a calculated risk on an exciting opportunity. This area rules education, so feed your hungry mind with a stimulating class or workshop.

January 31: Leo full moon (total lunar eclipse & supermoon)

Today's rare second full moon in January is a powerful, potentially game-changing total eclipse (and supermoon). Because it lands in your communication house, you're being invited to express yourself fully and honestly. Whether in person or online, your ideas could go viral, so be sure you've got all your facts straight.

February: Love Hotspots

February 4: Venus-Jupiter square

Get the facts before you react. Jumping to conclusions prematurely could stir up drama. Avoid being a know-it-all or dishing out unsolicited advice to your partner. If someone tries to "fix" you, that could be a red flag. What ever happened to unconditional love?

February 10-March 6: Venus in Pisces

Today kicks off a tender and compassionate four weeks as the love planet pays her annual visit to your tenth house of long-range goals. So, what do you want for the future, whether with your longtime love or a new (or potential) partner? Knowing is the first big step toward manifesting it!

February 21: Venus-Neptune meetup

In the middle of her tour of Pisces and your future-oriented zone, Venus meets up with wistful Neptune, dialing up the emotions and the fantasy factor. While it's fine to dream up romantic plans, make sure you and the other person are on the same page. Otherwise, you could be in for a bit of a letdown.

February 25: Venus-Mars square

In the first of this year's three entanglements between the love planets, your romantic plans could get derailed. Bellicose Mars could fuel pressure to commit before you feel ready or spark a fight over something that shouldn't be an issue in the first place. Breathe!

February: Career Hotspots

February 10: Sun-Jupiter square

Watch out for FOMO under this star-crossed face-off. Sure, you want to do/see/have more, but you don't want to rush into something before you have a plan for managing it. Before you agree to anything, be sure you have an idea of how it'll work and, ideally, a competent support team in place.

February 13: Mercury-Jupiter square

When supersizer Jupiter faces off with analytical

Mercury, you could overthink things and overpromise. You might feel overwhelmed by TMI or confused by sketchy plans. Really consider what you're signing on for, since someone might be misrepresenting the situation.

February 15: Aquarius new moon (partial solar eclipse)

Chinese Year of the Dog

The new moon—intensified by a partial solar eclipse—in your ninth house of travel, study and entrepreneurship sets up a six-month phase of growth. You could get serious about a big startup idea for a startup or explore a return to school. Today also kicks off the Chinese Year of the Earth Dog, which is known to be communicative, serious, loyal and responsible about work.

February 17-March 6: Mercury in Pisces

Mental Mercury blasts into your tenth house of work and public image today, launching an ambitious new phase. Over the next three weeks, you may come up with a strategy for becoming more visible in your field, or just around the office. If you get the opportunity to speak publicly, face your fears and do it! Or, just get more vocal in meetings or with prospecting clients. Toot your own horn (humbly) a little. If you don't share your achievements with the world, how will anyone know about them?

February 17: Mars-Neptune square

Mars gives you the drive to take action, but thanks to a square with nebulous Neptune, the plan might not be as viable as it seems. Someone could be talking a big game but doesn't have the substance to follow through. Dig deeper, and don't be afraid to ask for more solid evidence.

February 25: Mercury-Neptune meetup

Your secret weapons at work today are your imagination and intuition. Creative visualization can help you manifest future plans and goals, especially if you're feeling stymied.

February 28: Mercury-Mars square

Don't rush into partnering up or sharing your trade secrets. Mars can spark rash action, but you'll benefit from taking the time to think things through. Make sure your core needs are met before you team up. If you're not happy with the terms, negotiate!

March: Love Hotspots

March 1: Venus-Jupiter trine

These two "benefics" (positive planets) form a stabilizing trine, giving a solid structure to your relationship. If there's something you've been wanting to say, you'll have cosmic support today. Single? Keep your eyes open at work or career-related activities. Romance is in the air!

March 1: Virgo full moon

The year's only full moon of its kind falls in your sentimental fourth house, bringing emotions out into the open. It's okay—encouraged, even—to wear your heart on your sleeve and be vulnerable. Coupled Geminis may exchange keys, make plans to meet each other's families or have a moment of deep bonding.

March 4: Mercury-Venus meetup

When the communicator of the zodiac teams up with the love planet in romantic Pisces and your structured tenth house, you'll want to clarify boundaries and expectations with a partner. Are you on the same page about the future? Don't assume. Make your long-range goals clear, then be prepared to listen to theirs.

March 6-31: Venus in Aries
As the love planet sizzles in Aries and your sector of friendship and technology, single Geminis might consider offering a "benefits package" to a platonic pal, or you could strike up a stimulating online connection. Couples will enjoy socializing more with each other's friends—or you might need to be apart a little more to appreciate the time you do spend together!

March 13: Venus-Saturn square
You may feel pulled in two directions under today's bewildering aspect. Structured Saturn in your "playing for keeps" eighth house is all about commitment and the future, but the love planet is in impulsive Aries and your "keep it light" eleventh house. Better to stall on important decisions and just have fun with friends to distract yourself from this quandary.

March 17-May 16: Mars in Capricorn
Rash and robust Mars jets into your erotic eighth house for two months, stoking the lusty fires within. You could lunge into a steamy affair or be tempted by forbidden fruit. Since you may not be able to rein your desires in, just be honest with yourself about what you're getting into. If you're splitting up, things could get contentious, especially if you're dividing up shared property. Couples could fight about money or sex. Try to settle your differences in the bedroom.

March 23: Venus-Pluto square
Check in with your emotions today. You might be overreacting or simply unaware of how intensely you're coming off. What's really going on? Do you feel attacked or threatened? Call a time-out before you say or do something you'll live to regret.

March 31-April 24: Venus in Taurus
For the next three and a half weeks, the love planet will go subterranean as she hunkers down in your twelfth house of introspection and surrender. Drop your guard, open your heart and see what happens when you don't try to force or control things. Dancing with a new partner? Let them take the lead!

March 31: Libra full moon
Oh l'amour! The year's only full moon in your fifth house of glamour, lust and creativity is something to celebrate! This could bring a budding connection to the next level or inspire you to express your desires or honest feelings toward someone. Vulnerability can be a turn-on.

March: Career Hotspots

March 2: Mercury-Jupiter trine
These creative planets align in your grounded, work-oriented houses, inspiring you to go out on a limb and share some of your original ideas. Don't hold back now. This mashup may be the first step toward bringing you more recognition, a wider fanbase or market share.

March 4: Sun-Neptune meetup
The bold Sun and intuitive Neptune blend energies in your career corner today, adding pizazz and

sparkle to your words. People will be intrigued by what you have to say, so give them the whole story, not just the elevator pitch. Not sure how to proceed on a certain project? Close your door, tune in to your inner wisdom—and trust what comes!

March 6-May 13: Mercury in Aries

Your ruler, cerebral Mercury, grooves into your teamwork sector. Make the most of this extended opportunity to forge new professional alliances and "work across the aisle" with people from different departments or with dissimilar views. If you can come to a meeting of the minds, you might come up with something totally original and progressive!

March 11: Mars-Uranus trine

You and a colleague could inspire each other to do something a little out of the box today, and knowing you have each other's back gives you the confidence to give it a serious shot. Teamwork will make the dream work today!

March 11: Mercury-Saturn square

You're eager to try something new and untested, but you may bang up against closed-minded resistance from an associate or higher-up who insists on hard data before green-lighting this experiment. If you feel strongly, fight for it—strategically, of course.

March 13: Sun-Jupiter trine

The expressive Sun in your career zone gets a unanimous vote of confidence from expansive Jupiter in your productive sixth house, giving you exactly the support you need to tackle a big new project. Do you need some more hands on deck? Let people know what you're working on; they might climb over one another to sign on!

March 17: Pisces new moon

The year's only new moon in your career corner plants the seeds for a whole new trajectory—if you're looking to make a change. If you're happy with the status quo, this lunation will kick off a turbo-charged six-month cycle of professional growth and help you set some new goals for the coming year.

March 22-April 15: Mercury retrograde in Aries

Hurry up and wait! Today begins a three-week cycle of delays and confusion involving technology, communication and travel. Your ruler, mental Mercury, spins into retrograde motion in your group activities sector. Be circumspect about what you share with friends and colleagues. Not everyone has the most honorable intentions. Learning to be savvier is one of the great lessons of this period.

March 24: Sun-Mars square

Who's the boss? If you're not, back down from your insistence about…everything. You may have gotten a little carried away with your ideas (however brilliant they are). While it's important to stand up for yourself, consider it a red flag when you veer into obsessive, dictatorial territory.

March 29: Sun-Saturn square

If you feel yourself putting up the steel bars of your inner defense system, look at what's causing that. Are you truly under attack, or could some old fears around trust be raising their head? During this a one-day transit, it might be better to not engage with anyone until you sort things out.

     The AstroTwins' 2018 Gemini Planetary Planner

April: Love Hotspots

April 2: Mars-Saturn meetup

Self-discipline is called for today, but it may be in short supply as impulsive Mars teams up with restrained Saturn in your eighth house of intimacy and seduction. You may feel like you have to scratch that itch, but if you're playing the long game, it's better to hold out a bit. For couples, strong emotions could test your bond—and ultimately strengthen it. If a chronic issue comes to a head, you might not be able to work this out yourselves. It may be worth a few sessions with a therapist.

April 7: Venus-Saturn trine

You may get your wish today, as the love planet joins forces with structured Saturn in your eighth house of sex and intimacy. In a LTR? Don't try to do all the heavy lifting by yourself. Allow your partner to support you emotionally. Under this serious starmap, you could discuss serious stuff—engagement, moving in together, big financial decisions—in a way that feels bonding, not daunting.

April 11: Venus-Mars trine

Today has the potential to be one of the most romantic days of the year. Can you feel the love? If you can't, tune in. If you can, go deeper! The cosmic paramours, Venus and Mars, are aligned in your most emotional, intuitive houses. It's safe to let your guard down and bask in the glow of someone else's affection.

April 17: Venus-Jupiter opposition

Codependent interactions aren't always obvious, so stay on your guard today. With these planets at odds, somebody may act like they want to help, but it could be a power play. And check in with yourself. If you're the one attempting an emotionally manipulative move, stop yourself in your tracks.

April 17: Venus-Pluto trine

There's nothing casual about today's vibes. Venus in your subterranean zone aligns with smoldering Pluto in your eighth house of intimacy. You might feel compelled to bring up unfulfilled emotional needs or initiate a conversation about making things more official. Single? Stay open to different types. An appealing suitor might pursue you with big talk and fast moves.

April 24-May 19: Venus in Gemini

Get ready for a romantic power surge! The love planet embarks on her annual trek through your sign, imbuing you with magnetic sex appeal. Don't let it go to your head, though. If you've got a partner, be sure to keep strong the ties that bind.

April 26: Mars-Pluto meetup

It's a hot and heavy day—and that's putting it mildly. When these two intense, lusty planets align in your erotic eighth house, some serious chemistry is sure to get fired up!

April 29: Sun-Saturn trine

"Casual" could get serious today, as the ego-driven Sun aligns with commitment-minded Saturn. Single? Let your friends play matchmaker, and don't second-guess their choices until you give 'em a chance. Attached? Find a social group or charitable organization that speaks to both of your hearts.

April: Career Hotspots

April 1: Sun-Mercury meetup

Take command in a group setting by speaking your mind or championing a worthy cause. Your words carry a lot of weight today, and a powerful message you post could go viral. Need a testimonial or reference? Ask your well-connected allies to write one for you.

April 2: Mars-Saturn meetup

Slow down if you catch yourself rushing into a financial deal or joint venture. While you don't want to miss out on a solid opportunity, acting impulsively would be foolish (and potentially expensive). Gather the facts as quickly as you can; then choose wisely.

April 4: Mercury-Mars square

Don't expect to see eyeball-to-eyeball with everyone today, Gemini. Your ruler, cerebral Mercury, is retrograde, which can muddle a group project. You can always agree to disagree, but find out if you even share any of the same long-term goals.

April 11: Sun-Pluto square

There's strength in numbers, but also the potential for discord and dissent. Under this shadowy square, you may discover that someone on your team has ulterior motives or is only acting out of self-interest. If you feel held back by a group, focus on your own work or personal contributions.

April 15: Aries new moon

This new moon in your collaborative eleventh house connects you to a group of innovative thinkers and doers. You'd be honored to be a part of their organization, but be patient! Give yourself six months to see what your synergy can create.

April 18: Sun-Uranus meetup

Good teams allow people to let their unique talents shine. Turn up your light even as you work collectively on a project that can better the world.

April 25: Mercury-Saturn square

You might feel alone even though you're surrounded by team members today. If you feel out of step or as if people don't get the direction you're going in, perhaps it's a sign that you haven't thoroughly hashed out your ideas, and more research or due diligence is needed before you can seal the deal.

April 26: Mars-Pluto meetup

Today is ideal for strategy sessions and tactical moves. Strike with precision and impeccable timing! You might form a powerful alliance or team up with a well-connected person who can usher you into an elite and influential circle.

April 29: Scorpio full moon

The only Scorpio full moon of the year lands in your sixth house of work, service and helpful people. Have you been carrying too much of the load yourself? Delegating or outsourcing to the right person could be a wise investment. Over the next few weeks, focus on decluttering and reorganizing. You'll be more productive as a result.

     The AstroTwins' 2018 Gemini Planetary Planner

May: Love Hotspots

May 7: Venus-Neptune square

Looking for love in all the wrong places? Today, Venus in your sign faces off with dreamy Neptune in your future-oriented tenth house. Are you trying to fit a square peg into a round hole? If you don't have the same expectations, you could wind up hurt. And think twice about an office attraction. If it doesn't pan out, how will you handle the awkwardness?

May 15: Taurus new moon

It's time to move on—but first, what do you need to release? Today's new moon in your house of closure and healing supports you in shutting one door so a better one can open. Ask for forgiveness—or accept an apology—to clear the air. Then get on with your life.

May 15: Uranus in Taurus (until November 6)

This is Day One of a major planetary shift that is in effect until 2026. Transformative Uranus will be helping you understand your own emotions and inner life—but remember, this is a process, not something you can accomplish overnight.

May 16-August 12: Mars in Aquarius

Passionate Mars ziplines into your "try anything once (twice if you like it)" ninth house. You'll get an extra-long power surge in this area because the red planet is retrograde for much of the summer. This house also rules adventure and travel, so don't be surprised if you embark on a long-distance relationship.

May 16: Mars-Uranus square

Serendipity is your new favorite word, as unexpected connections develop and your attempts at manifesting hit pay dirt. Keep on paying attention to those "coincidental" signs from the universe—they're telling you something! But don't be too quick to interpret or act on them. You're prone to making rash moves in the heat of passion (or anger) under this fast-moving aspect.

May 19-June 13: Venus in Cancer

Solid as a rock! That's how you'll feel when the love planet grooves into your grounded second house for nearly a month. In affairs of the heart (and the wallet), you'll be craving more certainty. Treat your S.O. or a hot prospect to a bit of luxury, and let yourself be taken on more fancy, upscale dates.

May 25: Mercury-Pluto trine

You could be rolling in the deep with a new or true-blue partner under this depth-defying mashup. Open up and be prepared to share—or learn—something that's known by only a few people (if any).

May 26: Venus-Saturn opposition

A little caution goes a long way. Under this guarded face-off, you could wittingly (or not) erect a self-protective barrier with your beloved or a new prospect. Or just as you're ready to open up a bit, you feel like you're being ghosted. Be slow to merge financial resources under this restrained aspect.

May 29: Sagittarius full moon

The year's only full moon in your partnership house could bring a budding connection to a peak, or an ongoing union could finally reach a tipping point.

54

Before you take your next step, check in with your heart: Are you ready to go all in? Single Geminis could meet someone with long-term potential, so let your desires be known.

May: Career Hotspots

May 7: Mercury-Pluto square

People aren't being upfront, things may not be what they seem, and you could get sucked into a power struggle over something you thought was resolved. Be careful what you reveal, especially online. Update passwords and strengthen security settings to protect important data.

May 8: Sun-Jupiter opposition

Don't call for a slick sales pitch today. Someone could be painting a picture that's way rosier than the reality, and under this optimistic mashup, you'll want to buy into it. But seeing is believing, so take off the filtered lenses and have a clear-eyed look.

May 11: Sun-Pluto trine

With the ego-supporting Sun aligned with penetrating Pluto, you can't not speak from the heart. People will rally around your candor and integrity today, so if you start to lose your nerve, look to them to reinforce your courage.

May 13-29: Mercury in Taurus

This next month and a half is a time to turn inward and take stock of your inner workings. With the cerebral planet in your foggy yet creative twelfth house, you won't have your usual gift of gab, and may find it hard to organize your thoughts. This is a better time to develop a meditation practice or sharpen your visualization skills. Someone in your inner circle may have hidden motives, so keep confidential information to yourself.

May 13: Mercury-Uranus meetup

Acknowledge the efforts of your work team, but get ready to move onto something bigger and more personally rewarding. Today, Mercury and Uranus exit Aries and your collaboration zone and move into Taurus. Uranus will stay here for eight years, during which time you'll get increasingly comfortable expressing your unique ideas.

May 16-August 12: Mars in Aquarius

The passionate planet beams into your visionary zone for an extended visit. This is the time to take risks, plot some daring, expansive moves, and go big. You may do a lot of exciting travel during this time, and could take on long-distance clients or projects that are associated with the media, publishing or education.

May 16: Mars-Uranus square

Shift into an abundance mindset instead one of scarcity. There's enough of everything to go around (and then some). If someone on your work team or in your inner circle starts acting competitive or is unwilling to share their info, rise above their petty machinations.

May 18: Mercury-Saturn trine

Solidify your creative ideas by putting them into a plan. A little structure will give your intuition a matrix to work within. You could be guided to make an important move, so listen to your inner voice. A conversation with an experienced person or a mentor may help clarify your path.

         The AstroTwins' 2018 Gemini Planetary Planner

May 23: Mercury-Jupiter opposition

Think, plan, research—but don't take action today if you can help it. This muddling aspect can hatch grandiose yet impractical ideas. You'll overshoot the mark or try for too much too soon.

May 23: Sun-Mars trine

Your cerebral sign is usually a mental step ahead of everyone else, so if something is on the tip of your tongue, say it without worrying what others will think. Mars gives you the confidence to step boldly into the spotlight.

May 25: Jupiter-Neptune trine

This is the second in a trio of rare trines (the first was December 2017; the last comes on August 19) in which expansive Jupiter sends a supportive beam to compassionate Neptune in your career corner. Anything you do that has the potential to better the world can enrich both your life and your bank account. Service is a two-way street, so be sure to acknowledge those who've helped you; one day you may be in a position to return the favor.

May 29-June 12: Mercury in Gemini

When your ruling planet visits your sign every year, it's the perfect time to express your deepest dreams and most original ideas. Don't overthink it; just trust that it'll come out right.

May 29: Sagittarius full moon

It's a great day to advance partnerships, ink a deal or make an alliance official. Teaming up with others takes your efforts further. A joint endeavor could reach a turning point, with you either parting ways or celebrating a shared victory.

June: Love Hotspots

June 1: Venus-Jupiter trine

With the positive "benefic" planets in a harmonious angle, you'll feel the love today! You might be inspired to perform a random act of kindness or give your beloved (or someone you adore) a meaningful gift.

June 2: Venus-Neptune trine

The hits keep coming! Today's loving embrace of Venus and enchantress Neptune dials up your compassion and capacity for empathy. One of the nicest things you can do for someone you care about is to just listen and not try to "solve" or "fix" anything.

June 5: Venus-Pluto opposition

Passive-aggressive much? You might not realize what you're doing until someone points out that you're acting contrarian about…pretty much everything. Before you do real damage to an important relationship, take a look at your head-trippy behavior—and change it!

June 13-July 9: Venus in Leo

When the love planet makes her annual sojourn through your communication corner, the greatest aphrodisiac will be stimulating conversation! A meeting of the minds could lead to a uniting of the hearts. Single Geminis might meet someone at a local venue, so spend more time in your own 'hood!

June 14: Venus-Uranus square

You want security and excitement? That's a tall order. Before you do anything potentially regrettable, consider that this might be a sign that you're not happy with the status quo.

June 21: Venus-Mars opposition

You're feeling something—but is it love or lust? You may be torn between taking your sweet old time and speeding up the process. Explore the possibilities and you'll know what to do soon enough.

June 25: Venus-Jupiter square

When expansive Jupiter stretches the love planet's field of vision, you might feel overwhelmed by too many options. It's a nice problem to have, but it can make it hard to commit to one person. Don't obsess on something your partner says. That will only make both of you crazy!

June 26-August 27: Mars retrograde

Mars backtracks through Aquarius and your risk-taking ninth house until August 12, then retreats into cautious Capricorn and your intimate eighth house for the duration. Don't rush into—or out of—anything until after August 27. Scale back plans that have become unmanageable, and keep both eyes on your money. If you've rushed into anything serious, you might take a step back and pace yourself.

June 28: Capricorn full moon

This earthily sensual full moon in your intimacy zone blows the lid off your deepest desires. You may not be able to keep your feelings, or fantasies, to yourself. So why not go for it? That could lead to one of the sexiest days—and nights—of the year.

June: Career Hotspots

June 1: Mercury-Mars trine

Slow down! Sure, you're all revved about something, but you may be promising too much and moving too fast. Give your mind (and mouth) a rest today. At the very least, keep everything in the realm of blue-sky possibilities and don't rush to act on those brainstorms.

June 7: Sun-Neptune square

When hazy Neptune in your career corner squares the self-assured Sun in your sign, you could experience a crisis of confidence. What you thought was rock-solid may turn out to be totally unrealistic. People can flake out—or disappear—without so much as a word of explanation, leaving you holding the bag.

June 12-29: Mercury in Cancer

When the cosmic messenger wings into your second house of work and money, you're holding all the cards when it comes to negotiating, pitching new prospects or making a big ask. This is a good couple of weeks to review your budget and priorities.

June 13: Gemini new moon

Happy (personal) New Year! The year's only new moon in your sign heralds a time for new starts and hitting "refresh" on anything that hasn't achieved liftoff yet. No point looking back. Keep your eyes and your focus on what lies ahead, and feel empowered to pursue your most prized solo ventures.

June 26-August 27: Mars retrograde

When the action planet shifts into reverse, it's time

to slow your own forward motion. Are you dreaming a little too big? This is your "going back to the drawing board" opportunity, so take a clear-eyed look at your plans to see where you might benefit from scaling back or buying yourself a little more time.

June 27: Sun-Saturn opposition
It's financial reality-check time! Serious, structured Saturn sends a tough-love beam to the optimistic Sun, shedding undeniable light on where you've miscalculated monetarily. It's discouraging, yet also important to know that, with some new fiscal responsibility, you can pay down debt and start saving for those desired big purchases.

June 28: Capricorn full moon
A major alliance could come to fruition under this grounded moon. You may close a deal, ink a joint venture or make a savvy long-term investment. With your eighth house of property activated, real estate and legal matters will be in the spotlight over the coming few months.

June 29-September 5: Mercury in Leo
Thanks to a retrograde from July 26 to August 19, you'll have an extra-long period of hosting your celestial ruler in your innovative, expressive third house. Get your ideas out of your head and onto the table, where you can begin to turn them into a reality.

July: Love Hotspots

July 9-August 6: Venus in Virgo
Your nostalgic side comes out full force this summer. Open your heart; let your sensitive, sentimental side out. Ready for a next move with your S.O.?

This is a good four-week phase for making plans to meet families, moving in together or thinking about welcoming a baby.

July 11: Venus-Uranus trine
You could drop your emotional guard spontaneously, perhaps even sharing a deep, dark secret. Seeking love? You might meet a fantasy-sparking soulmate type out of the blue.

July 14: Venus-Saturn trine
Solid relationships can survive the occasional swells of stormy seas, so don't hit the panic button if you've been on the outs lately. This trine between grounded Saturn and loving Venus creates the perfect opportunity to hug it out—and talk it out, if one of you feels it's essential. Otherwise, let bygones be bygones.

July 24: Venus-Neptune opposition
Under this emotionally foggy aspect, you may feel confused or misled in a relationship, so hold off making any life-altering decisions today. One (or both) of you might be acting out of old wounds without realizing it.

July 27: Venus-Pluto trine
Go deep in the name of love today. You can take a union to a whole new level by sharing from the heart.

July: Career Hotspots

July 5: Mercury-Mars opposition
It'll be easy to criticize or act like an annoying know-it-all, but rein yourself in. Under this tricky transit, there's likely to be information you aren't

aware of. Lead with compassion. You yourself might be feeling extra sensitive, so don't go soliciting feedback. Chances are, you'll be a little too thin-skinned to hear it right now.

July 5: Sun-Jupiter trine

Nothing wrong with a paycheck, but you need to know that, on some level, your work is improving people's lives and giving some significance to yours. If it's not, is there another way you could find that kind of fulfillment?

July 8: Sun-Neptune trine

This is a powerful day for manifesting—especially involving work or partnerships that can actually make a difference in people's lives. What can you do with your own money that gives back or pays it forward?

July 9: Mercury-Jupiter square

There's a reason they say "keep it simple." When you veer into overanalysis (like today), you truly lose sight of the big picture. Wherever you are, hit pause and reframe your perspective. No sense moving forward without a clear mindset.

July 12: Sun-Pluto opposition

There's potentially a lot of money to be made in a joint deal but also a lot of risk. Under this shadowy sync-up, someone may be withholding information or misrepresenting the facts. Be slow to react to proposals and get all of the facts first. Then take a few days to think things over before responding. Do you sense a power struggle brewing? Move to the sidelines and regroup.

July 12: Cancer new moon (partial solar eclipse)

This annual event could bring some exciting money news, a job offer or a fresh approach to fiscal security. Over the coming six months, you may turn your finances around, change careers or launch a side business that creates a nicely flowing revenue stream.

July 25: Sun-Uranus square

You may be tempted to fire off an angry email or give someone an unedited piece of your mind, but hold your stallions. Uranus is prompting rash action, but since it's squaring the Sun in your communication corner, you could wind up eating those words in the not-so-distant future. Go ahead and put it in writing—just don't dream of actually sending that feisty proclamation!

July 26-August 19: Mercury retrograde in Leo

Here we go again! Messenger Mercury, ruler of expression and technology, kicks off a three-week backspin, this time through Leo and your communication house. You could pull your hair out—or you may take it as a divine signal to practice patience and become more cautious about what you say or put in writing.

July 27: Aquarius full moon (total lunar eclipse)

Ideas and projects you've been working on for the past six months could come to fruition now. This "full-circle" full moon rewards hard work and can catapult you to the next level. La luna in your ninth house of travel, education and entrepreneurship, might help you make a bold change to pursue one (or more) of these areas. Take a gamble on a stimulating initiative and follow your bliss.

July 27: Sun-Mars opposition

Hold your fire, Gemini! Someone might get your ire up, but that doesn't give you permission to go off on them. Bellicose Mars is primed for a fight, but unless you're willing to totally cut ties with this person, distract yourself, redirect and revisit the situation in another day or so, when cooler heads will prevail.

August: Love Hotspots

August 6-September 9: Venus in Libra

Feeling hot, hot, hot! Enjoy this sultry spell of hosting demonstrative Venus in your flirty and passionate fifth house. Whether or not you're spoken for, this five-week phase could be the highlight of your romantic year.

August 7: Venus-Mars trine

When the love planets hook up, you're sure to do the same. This is a super-lucky day for romancing, and possibly in a surprising way. Single friends may become lovers, partners could part ways amicably and become friends—or take things to an exciting new level.

August 9: Venus-Saturn square

You may feel conflicted in your love life under this uneasy face-off. The Venus side wants to flirt and reveal your true feelings, but cautious Saturn is pulling back on the reins—hard. Ask yourself: What's the best and most honest way to get your romantic needs met?

August 12-September 10: Mars in Capricorn

The red-hot planet retreats into Capricorn for the rest of its retrograde, going direct (forward) here on August 27. While the cosmic provocateur is in your eighth house of intense emotions, you may spend time processing some deep-seated issues that involve trust and intimacy. If you're in a relationship, conflicts could erupt simply by your partner looking at you wrong. Watch your temper, and if you do go mano a mano, make sure you fight fair!

August 25: Sun-Saturn trine

This isn't about what he said or she said. Trying to explain or rationalize your feelings will get you nowhere fast. Instead, dig in deeper and just share what's in your heart, however messily it comes out.

August 26: Venus-Pluto square

Keep it light and breezy? Good luck with that. With manipulative Pluto in the mix, you're more interested in revenge of the "going for the jugular" variety. But that's a slippery slope. Can you vent to a friend or your journal and not approach this person until tomorrow, when the heat of the moment passes? Try.

August 27: Mars retrograde ends

Can we get an amen? The passionate planet concludes his frustrating two-month retrograde that began June 26. Now he's back in fifth gear, motoring forward in your sexy and erotic eighth house. Here Mars will do what he does best— crank up the heat in your love life—but watch out! With more fiery intensity comes an uptick in anger, jealousy and possessiveness.

August: Career Hotspots

August 2: Mars-Uranus square

It's hard to "expect" the unexpected, but under today's wildly unpredictable skies, that's the only way to roll. The good news for you is that this cosmic clash will shake up your imagination—in a good way. Trust ideas that come from out of the blue. These cosmic downloads are definitely worth exploring.

August 6: Sun-Jupiter square

Just when you thought it was safe to go back in the water…"someone" starts blowing hot air and/or making promises they can't keep. People may be thin-skinned and quick to criticize, yet unwilling (or unable) to look at themselves. The best way to stay out of the fray is to keep a low profile—and your opinions to yourself.

August 10: Mercury-Jupiter square

Take a cue from the late beat poet Allen Ginsberg, who succinctly said, "First thought, best thought." Too much analysis will tie you up in knots and make reaching a decision impossible.

August 11: Leo new moon (partial solar eclipse)

A potent new moon that's also a solar eclipse spurs some major changes in your social sphere. You won't be caught sitting around trying to figure out what to do next. You could get deeply involved in a worthwhile cause or spearhead a local cultural event. Stay open to "random conversations"; you never know where they'll lead!

August 12-September 10: Mars in Capricorn

Woo-hoo! Driven Mars returns to your eighth house of investments and shared finances, giving you the get-up-and-go to earn more and make your money work harder for you. Just one catch: Mars is retrograde until August 27, which can create tension and conflict around those joint ventures. Avoid doing anything impulsive or without consensus.

August 19: Jupiter-Neptune trine

Expansive Jupiter forms the third in a trio of rare trines to compassionate Neptune in your career corner. (The first was on December 2, 2017; the second was on May 25.) Work is about so much more than a paycheck and now, inspired by this transcendent alignment, you may seek out projects that serve humankind. Show your appreciation for the support "staff" in your life who are as responsible for your success and sense of satisfaction as anyone.

August 26: Pisces full moon

This annual event inspires you to raise the bar on your goals and really go for the gold (silver and bronze just won't do it!). This full moon in your ambitious tenth house could bring a huge opportunity or recognition. If your present professional path isn't fulfilling enough, you'll have the courage to make a bold change.

August 27: Mars retrograde ends

Long-term finances, especially shared ventures, have been especially trying, either moving too quickly (hello, meltdown!) or stalled in a holding pattern. This may have led to chronic low-grade (or intense) stress. But now that competitive Mars is moving forward, the challenges should finally clear up.

August 28: Mercury-Jupiter square

Time for a do-over? This is a repeat performance of these two superstars' mashup, but this time, communicator Mercury is not retrograde, which could make for an easier time. Still, you're full of fiery feelings, and if you're not careful, your strong opinions might land you in some seriously hot water.

September: Love Hotspots

September 7: Mercury-Uranus trine

This is an auspicious day to speak openly about your feelings or to forgive and move on already. Someone close to you could offer helpful words of wisdom. You may realize that it's better to offer a dose of compassion than a serving of tough love. Doing so might make a big difference for your bond.

September 8: Venus-Mars square

With the love planets on the outs today, your emotions could be a little raw and right on the surface. It won't take much for your feelings to get hurt, so keep a low profile, and whatever you do, don't pick a fight with your S.O. or love interest.

September 9-October 31: Venus in Scorpio

The love goddess arrives in your sixth house of wellness and organization for an extra-long spell thanks to a retrograde that begins on October 5. During this time, you might decide to simplify your life and try to be sensible about love. Single Geminis could meet someone through healthy pursuits. Couples may adopt a pet or start working out together more regularly.

September 9: Virgo new moon

This annual event, which lands in your emotional fourth house, can make your home and family the center of your attention for the coming six months. Some Geminis might embark on a sensitive and sentimental new chapter—or up and move long-distance for love. Soon you could be exchanging keys, talking babies or just opening up about your feelings a little more.

September 10-November 15: Mars in Aquarius

Lusty Mars makes its second trip this year through your adventurous and worldly ninth house—this time, for a retrograde-free journey. A cross-cultural attraction could heat up or you could meet someone while traveling, studying or doing something way out of your comfort zone.

September 11: Sun-Pluto trine

The intense meetup of these deep-diving planets in the most vulnerable and private parts of your chart encourages you to reveal more of your true feelings and share from the heart. People don't love you because you're "perfect"; they're attracted to your authentic, human, vulnerable side. Connect from there.

September 12: Venus-Uranus opposition

Under these unpredictable skies, you could receive some surprising information that might cause you to react impulsively or retreat in confusion. Not knowing where you stand can be more disruptive and destabilizing than getting bad but clear news. Avoid doing anything irreversible or trying to manipulate others to get a firmer footing.

September 18: Mars-Uranus square

When these rash, headstrong planets butt heads for the third time, there's no telling what you might get into. Before you do anything too dramatic—like act on a sketchy or clandestine attraction—try to project into the future and imagine the worst-case-scenario consequences.

September 21-October 9: Mercury in Libra

From your passionate, romantic fifth house, the communication planet offers a fashion tip: Wear your heart on your sleeve. You shouldn't stuff down your desires or hide your feelings now—nor will you be able to!

September 25: Sun-Saturn square

Is someone getting too close too fast? The expressive Sun in your romance house clashes with cautious Saturn. If you feel like a new love interest is trying to overstep a boundary, say something. Or you may be concerned that a budding relationship isn't getting off the ground quickly enough. Patience, Gemini! Enjoy the sweet, slow buildup. Regardless of what happens, you won't get to experience that again!

September: Career Hotspots

September 5-21: Mercury in Virgo

With your ruling planet jetting through your sensitive fourth house, you should feel free to express your feelings more openly and lead with your heart instead of your head. If you need to make a big ask or lead a pitch meeting, use creativity and emotion to be persuasive instead of bone-dry facts.

September 7: Sun-Neptune opposition

Newsflash: There is a line between your professional and personal lives, and no matter how blurry nebulous Neptune can make it, it's up to you to set some boundaries and then enforce them. If you're spending more time at work or with your colleagues than your loved ones, hit the refresh button. You may need to assert yourself a few times until it sinks in, but eventually the powers that be will get it. (The question is: Will you?)

September 10-November 15: Mars in Aquarius

The red planet returns for a second (this time, retrograde-free) trip through your expansive ninth house. It's time to get your ticket punched for a ride on the indie business train! Ambitious Mars here can also spark a return to education or send you packing your bags on a dream trip or dabbling in publishing. For the next two months, the world really does feel like your oyster!

September 18: Mars-Uranus square

Honesty is a good policy, but speaking too bluntly could provoke a passive-aggressive backlash. Keep your more incendiary opinions to yourself or be prepared to deal with hotheaded explosions and people taking their issues out on you.

September 24: Aries full moon

The full moon illuminates your teamwork zone, signaling that a group project could hit a tipping point or reach a successful finale. Aries brings new beginnings, so you might be parting ways with one crew and moving on to a new one.

> "Cerebral Mercury, ruler of communication, wings into your orderly and detail-minded sixth house. This is a brilliant three-week phase to get your life in order. "

September 27: Sun-Mars trine

Go big or go home! This action-oriented alignment is perfect for launching a bold initiative or doing anything that takes guts. A calculated risk will shine a light on a part of your personality you don't always show. You'll be able to express yourself with confidence and charisma, so put your personal stamp on that visionary project and shop it around.

October: Love Hotspots

October 2: Mercury-Pluto square

You might have the urge to merge, but for your own protection, don't reveal your whole hand to someone until they've earned your trust. Be mindful of what you say—and how you say it—to avoid accidentally poking sensitive spots and provoking unnecessary drama.

October 5-November 16: Venus retrograde

The love planet reverses course in Scorpio until October 31 before retreating into Libra and your romance corner, where it can disrupt the harmony between you and your amour du jour. Don't let emotions get out of control, especially your anger. This backflip may bring the return of an ex. Remind yourself of all the reasons you're no longer together! Or, if you give it another go, explore with the utmost caution.

October 8: Libra new moon

This annual event in your courtship corner offers the chance for a fresh start in love. Give some different types a fair shot this time around. Attached? Put more effort into dressing up and going out together. You may not think it makes a difference, but watch. Couples who are trying to conceive could have luck, as this new moon falls in your fertility house.

October 9-31: Mercury in Scorpio

Cerebral Mercury, ruler of communication, wings into your orderly and detail-minded sixth house. This is a brilliant three-week phase to get your life in order. Attack those chores and admin tasks that you've been putting off, as well as anything that requires an eagle eye. It's also a good time to check your financial accounts and do some project management.

October 10: Venus-Mars square

Can you resist anything but temptation, Gemini? You might need to lock yourself up today, as the enticing vibes are strong, and emotions could be hard to get a handle on. You could be enticed to explore an attraction, even though one (or both) of you might not be available. Careful!

October 12: Sun-Pluto square

You could be minding your own business when—wham!—a power struggle erupts. Is someone overstepping their bounds? If you're the one whose emotions are out of control, look deep beneath the surface. What you think is bothering you may not be even close to what's really going on.

October 24: Taurus full moon

This once-a-year major event lands in your twelfth house of fantasy, closure and healing and could trigger some strong feelings. Solid couples might feel closer as a result, but this may be the nail in the coffin for unstable unions.

October 31: Venus-Uranus opposition

Uncertainty can be harder to deal with than a challenging situation because you don't know where you stand. This tough face-off could cause you to act impulsively or in a controlling way, but check in with yourself to see if this is just triggering some old fears. Talk it out with a friend or therapist—anything to avoid doing something regrettable.

October 31-December 2: Venus in Libra

And she's back! Affectionate Venus reprises her August visit to your passionate fifth house, giving you a rare second chance with someone that didn't work out the first time around. Maybe you both had some growing up to do, or one of you wasn't available. Now you can give it a fair shot. Attached? This is an opportunity to work through some of the "same old" conflicts with a fresh approach. Dial down the drama and explore those lusty longings with both eyes open, though. Venus is still retrograde until November 16, which could bring a couple more bumpy spots.

October: Career Hotspots

October 2: Mercury-Pluto square

Discretion, please! With shadowy Pluto clashing with the communication planet, be extra cautious about what you say. Hold some (if not all) of your cards close to your vest. People may be far more calculating than they seem, so feel out their intentions before you reveal yours.

October 10: Mercury-Uranus opposition

It'll be easy to blurt under this loose-lipped face-off, but resist! It's essential that you think before you speak, because a slip of the tongue could be costly. Stay focused and conscious: Conversations may become upsetting quickly, with people lashing out and making critical, mean-spirited remarks. Don't stoop to their level!

October 19: Mercury-Neptune trine

Bring some heart and soul to the office—but stay focused on what needs to get done! It's possible to be compassionate and still hold others accountable. Speak softly and carry a big checklist.

October 24: Sun-Uranus opposition

Good luck trying to bring order to the Gemini court. Attempts to keep things under control may not amount to much as others' hidden agendas come to light and disrupt your best-laid plans. It's not going to be easy, but today your job is to strike the right balance between power and surrender, even if that means vacillating between them.

October 29: Mercury-Jupiter meetup

Bring your most stupefying problems to the table today. Under this genius-making mashup, your

 The AstroTwins' 2018 Gemini Planetary Planner

mind is razor-sharp. Don't waste it on Sudoku and social media; turn instead to strategic big-picture planning and visioning.

November: Love Hotspots

November 8, 2018–December 2, 2019: Jupiter in Sagittarius

The thrill is back! Today marks the beginning of a super-fabulously lucky love year, as expansive Jupiter takes the first step of its 13-month trek through your seventh house of committed partnerships. This lovely transit brings positive, extensive energy to every kind of alliance, from creative to professional to romantic!

November 9: Venus-Mars trine

Under this magnificent meetup of the cosmic lovers, your heart is overflowing with passion and optimism. Vixen Venus proffers the charisma to attract a suitable suitor, and Mars gives the drive to pursue back! Attached? Start planning your dream adventure or vacation.

November 15: Mars in Pisces

Blast off! You're on the fast track to making a commitment official or locking down a future plan. With Mars revving up the pace, you could feel pressure to seal a deal or agree to something before you're 100 percent ready. Examine your resistance: Do you truly feel rushed, or might that be some legitimate fears cropping up?

November 16-December 6: Mercury retrograde

Communicator Mercury begins its retreat in your relationship house before reversing into Scorpio and your health zone on December 1. This isn't the best time to talk through any conflicts you're experiencing with a partner, as you might be at cross-purposes. Tensions mount, pouring fuel on the fire. Wait it out. After December 6, it'll be much easy to express yourself!

November 16: Venus retrograde ends

Right as the communication planet starts its backspin, harmonizer Venus ends hers. Since November 5, the love planet has been loopy, which may have sparked drama or discord in your personal life. Hopefully, her direct (forward) turn will balance out some of the Mercury mayhem, and help you get back on the same harmonious page.

November 26: Sun-Jupiter meetup

It's dynamic duo time! The generous Sun swings into its only conjunction of the year with lucky Jupiter in your seventh house of committed relationships. If you've been thinking about teaming up with someone for work or creative purposes, this is one giant, cosmic green light. Romantically, it's even more exciting. If you're unattached, stay open to very different types. You can meet someone who, despite cultural differences, really gets you, and it's thrilling. Coupled up? Do something special tonight, something that has a sentimental meaning for you.

November 30: Venus-Uranus opposition

Are you or someone close to you playing mind games? So frustrating! One minute it's all "come closer"; the next you feel like a ghost. Sit this round out, and wait till this distancing transit passes tomorrow.

November: Career Hotspots

November 6, 2017–March 7, 2019: Uranus in Aries

As the unpredictable planet reverse-commutes into Aries and your eleventh house of group activity (before departing for good next March), your inner circle gets one last makeover. This zone rules technology, making this a perfect time to revamp your social media image.

November 7: Scorpio new moon

You can really home in on the nitty-gritty during this annual event that spotlights your sixth house of work, service and organization. Stop believing you have to do everything yourself! It may finally be time to get a wiz-kid intern or outsource the least exciting yet time-consuming parts of your work.

November 8, 2018–December 2, 2019: Jupiter in Sagittarius

Bring on the powerful partnerships! Teaming up with like-minded (or way more skillful and connected) people is your new formula for success. With expansive Jupiter kicking off a 13-month tour of your collaboration corner, there's no telling what you can accomplish when you merge your superpowers. Gemini, you could finally find your Wonder Twin. Let that be music to your ears!

November 15: Mars in Pisces

As the motivation maestro blasts into your ambitious tenth house for the rest of the year, you'll be on fire. You've got the drive, inspiration and energy to reach some of your biggest professional goals. Don't slow down till you get there!

November 19: Mars-Jupiter square

You could hit a roadblock on your race to the top. It may slow you down or force you to take a different route, but it's not going to stop you. You know exactly where you want to go, so stay focused on the goal and don't worry about a couple minor impasses.

November 23: Gemini full moon

The year's only full moon in your sign arrives like a half-birthday present. This once-a-year event lands in your first house of self, solo ventures and assertiveness. It's a powerful day, and as it shines the spotlight on you, give 'em all something to talk about!

December: Love Hotspots

December 2: Venus in Scorpio

When the love planet saunters into your sixth house—where she'll stay for the rest of the year—your attention turns to the areas associated with that sector, especially wellness and service. You'll take delight in helping others and being more of a giver than a receiver. Couples may get inspired to eat cleaner and greener and do more outdoorsy things together. Single? You could meet someone at yoga or doing volunteer work.

December 5: Sun-Neptune square

Looks (and desires) can be deceiving under this hazy planetary hookup. You think you know what you want, but you may be driven by ego and the need for constant praise—which isn't a solid foundation to base a relationship on, obviously. If you do meet someone today, take your time getting to know them. Couples will enjoy a warm fuzzy glow—but don't commit to any major next steps right now.

December 7: Sagittarius new moon

This annual event, which activates your relationship house, can start writing a new chapter in your love life or deepen an existing union. If you're feeling a little hemmed in, initiate a convo about how you can both pursue your interests without making the other feel abandoned.

December 7: Mars-Neptune meetup

Bold Mars aligns with fantasy-fueling Neptune in your future-oriented tenth house. Be careful not to get carried away with your dreams. You may be overly motivated AND unrealistic at the same time. This is a good time to clarify what you're looking for in a partner if you're single. Attached? Play up the fantasy side by trying something really out of the box.

December 12: Mercury in Sagittarius

Communicator Mercury returns for a sequel in your relationship corner and sticks around for the rest of the year. You'll be able to articulate your needs to your partner without coming off as needy or demanding. Be sure to ask them to share similar feelings. Single Geminis can count on your gift of gab to help break the ice with intriguing prospects. Chat up people with LTR potential and send the players moving along.

December 21: Venus-Neptune trine

This sweet sync-up puts you in loving, generous spirits. If you're in a relationship, be extra demonstrative and supportive of your mate, even if that means putting your own needs on the backburner for a bit. Since Neptune rules fantasy, feel free to share one that you've been keeping under wraps!

December: Career Hotspots

December 1: Mercury in Scorpio

Articulate Mercury has been retrograde for the past two weeks, and today it backflips into Scorpio, your orderly and analytical sixth house. You might not be able to make forward progress, but you can clean up some messes! Take on a decluttering mission and maybe "curate" your closet, taking all those gently worn items to charity, and the better ones to a consignment shop.

December 2: Sun-Mars square

Watch out for an explosive (and unpremeditated) power struggle with an authority figure or close collaborator at work. You may not see eye-to-eye around long-term goals, and as a result there could be a *Game of Thrones*-worthy battle of wills.

December 5: Sun-Neptune square

Keep a tighter grip on reality today. Your "grand goals" may be driven by ego and a need to be admired. With hazy Neptune in your career corner, you might not be seeing a certain situation clearly. Talk to a colleague for an objective assessment and, if necessary, correct course!

December 6: Mercury retrograde ends

You should have a much easier time getting organized and back on track with work or a fitness plan that got shunted to the sidelines. If you need to hire or fire someone, you can make a clear-headed decision now. Even better? Stress levels will decrease, and it won't be a struggle to get on the same page with people.

"The year wraps up on a big-money note as the only Cancer full moon of 2018 brings all your efforts of the past six months to a culmination point."

December 7: Sagittarius new moon

This once-a-year event falls in your dynamic duos zone and could spark a profitable new partnership, or you might be offered an appealing contract before the year is through. Unless there's a need to jump on it, take your time exploring the specifics. This new moon influences a six-month window, and some things need a while to fully unfold. Look at ways you can better balance the give-and-take in all your relationships now.

December 20: Sun-Uranus trine

People are your best assets today. If you can cede control and make sure others are playing to their strengths, you'll be on a winning team. Set an example by getting down in the trenches with everyone and recognizing what makes them unique—and what makes them tick. Now that's how to motivate people!

December 21: Mercury-Jupiter meetup

Under these mentally agile skies, you'll have no trouble negotiating a partnership or brainstorming with visionary and like-minded souls. With optimistic Jupiter in the equation, you can discuss really big ideas and engage in some blue-sky dreaming. But don't be too quick to act on anything, even if someone's eager to seal the deal. You need to be sure you have all the facts.

December 22: Cancer full moon

The year wraps up on a big-money note as the only Cancer full moon of 2018 brings all your efforts of the past six months to a culmination point. You could get the answer you've been waiting for, or, if you're lucky, be cashing a nice bonus check before you've even made your New Year's resolutions.

December 24: Mercury-Neptune square

Bah humbug! Someone doesn't seem to realize it's Christmas, because they're still trying to come to a resolution about that issue. Everyone else is ready to get their holiday on…so stop engaging! Realistically, nothing's going to happen until next week at the earliest, so put this out of your mind and go sing a few carols and spread some good cheer! ✸

2018

Numerology

THE 11/2 UNIVERSAL YEAR

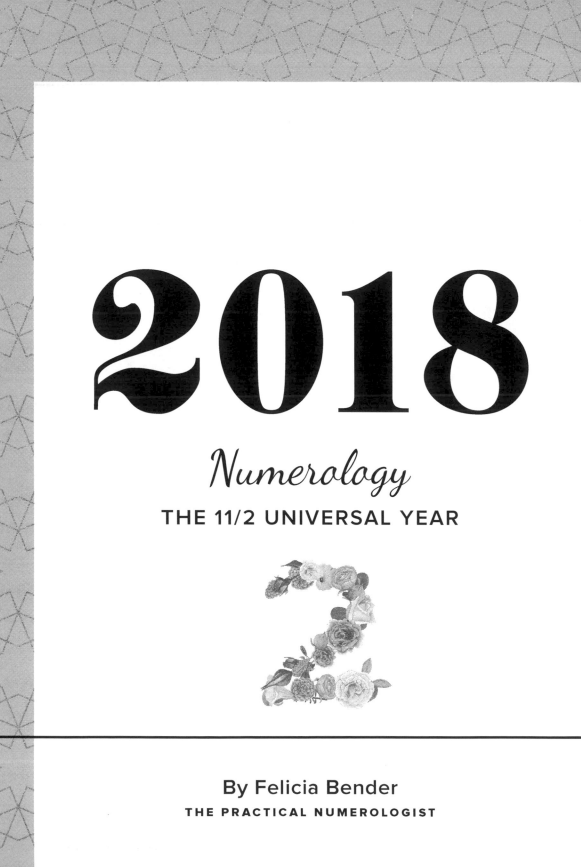

By Felicia Bender

THE PRACTICAL NUMEROLOGIST

The 11/2 Universal Year

HOW THIS "MASTER NUMBER" YEAR WILL TEACH US LOVE AND TOLERANCE

What is a Universal Year?

In Numerology, each calendar year adds up to a single-digit number, which holds a unique vibration. We all feel this energy, and it's called the Universal Year. A Universal Year means that everyone on the planet will experience the energy of a particular number during the entire year, from January 1 until December 31.

In Numerology, there are Universal Years and Personal Years. The Universal Year is like the landscape or terrain you're driving through all year long.

It's calculated by adding the numbers of the current year (in this case, 2018) together like this:

2018 = 2 + 0 + 1 + 8 = 11

11 is a "Master number" in Numerology (so make a note of that!)

Then reduce again: 1 + 1 = 2

Based on that equation, 2018 is a 2 Universal Year. And to add a special twist, the numbers 11, 22, 33 and 44 are called Master numbers in Numerology. So the world will experience a powerful 11/2 Universal Year.

Some numerologists never reduce the Master numbers and so this would be an 11 Universal Year. Other numerologists indicate the Master numbers by writing it as 11/2.

You also have a Personal Year number that changes each year. It's calculated from your individual birth date and tells you what you'll personally experience during the year.

Think of the Universal Year as the state or country you're driving through on your yearly "road trip" and the Personal Year as the points of destination you stop at as you travel through the year.

About the 11/2 Universal Year

Get ready for a year of spiritual illumination: 2018 is fueled by the Master number 11. The Master numbers carry a higher frequency, vibration and spiritual purpose. Energetically speaking, they're always pushing us deeper into self-realization and self-actualization. A Master number demands that we expand and evolve. Often, that process will be catalyzed by drama: extreme events or intensified circumstances.

The key is to understand what the foundational energy of the 2 brings to our year and then to see what the Master number 11 adds to the mix.

       The AstroTwins' 2018 Gemini Planetary Planner

"Eleven is the number of spiritual illumination. The number 11 resembles a doorway and acts a threshold to evolved consciousness."

The core energy of the year resides in the number 2. Without the Master number 11, the 2 Universal Year is a slower and patience-building time. Its energy offers delays and some frustrations along the way. It's a year to focus more on others than on ourselves. This is a change from 2017, which was a 1 Universal Year that put the spotlight on our personal needs and solo ventures.

The 2 Universal Year focuses on love, emotions and relationships. The energy of the 2 Universal Year takes the spotlight off of "you" flying solo and places the focus instead on "us" and what partnership means to our lives. The energy of the 2 Universal Year supports slowing down, becoming more social and getting intimate with our emotions.

This year we're upping the ante with the Master number 11/2. The 11 is a double 1—which is all about the self, independence, innovation and confidence. We just experienced a 1 Universal Year in 2017—an initiating year of rebirth, new beginnings and action. Yet, the foundational energy for the 11 is the 2, which is all about love, relating to others, partnership, patience and being supportive. Combined with the solo-driven energy of the 11, it can be a real paradox!

From 2015 to 2017, the world experienced a three-year transition cycle, comprised of the Universal Years 8, 9 and 1. Now 2018 brings a moment to rest and regroup—fueled by the 2 Universal Year number. It's a great year for getting to know ourselves better. With the diplomatic and loving 2 at play, intuition and sensitivity is heightened. Explore your emotions instead of distracting yourself with busy-ness.

The overall mission during this 11/2 Universal Year is to work together with harmony, balance and mutual respect. It's not always easy, but think of it this way: "Master" means "Teacher." The Master numbers prod all of us to "master" our lives in ways that are more elevated than usual. When you work with a Master number, it's as though you're enrolled in an academy for the gifted. Now it's time to open our textbooks and begin the school year.

Eleven is the number of spiritual illumination. The number 11 visually resembles a doorway and it acts a threshold to evolved consciousness. The energy offers deep and profound healing at a core level. This "healing" might not be apparent from the outside. It's a shift in perspective that changes us from within. This year, we can use our creativity and insight for the benefit of humanity.

Opportunities of the 11/2 Universal Year

Hurry up and wait? 2018 will be a year of action, but there will be delays and weird detours. It's like the urgency you feel when applying for a new job or starting a business. You need a plan, proper financing and the tenacity to go with the flow of creation—which is rarely (if ever) a linear path.

72

The trick will be in our collective ability to step back and develop new solutions and mindsets, and to find confidence in the face of change and uncertainty.

Balance autonomy and partnership. The double 1's offer twice the pleasure and the challenges related to the number 1. This year continues to push all of us to step into our power, express our individuality and exert healthy independence. And we have to do this while playing well with others.

Find your tribe. Detach from draining people and invest in relationships that inspire you to be your best self. Cultivating a support system takes time, so it won't happen overnight. Be patient and keep at it.

Balance masculine and feminine. Concern for humanity or "me first"? Inclusion or exclusion? The 2 is heart/feminine energy, while the double 1's are cerebral/masculine energy. An 11/2 Universal Year highlights these dualities. 2018 will challenge all of us to find the right balance between giving and receiving.

Challenges of the 11/2 Universal Year

An 11/2 year can deliver challenging circumstances that are help build character. If we pass these tests, we'll emerge stronger, more spiritually evolved and ready to assist others. Illumination comes when we find ourselves in darkness and opt for the light. This could be a year when we experience the "butterfly effect" firsthand, fighting our way out of chaos into clarity.

Be tolerant. A Master number cycle can heighten anxiety. Knowing this, we can be kinder to ourselves and more compassionate to others throughout the year. Remember that everyone is feeling this stress—not just you.

Embrace the lessons of conflict. The number 2 is the teacher of love, patience and diplomacy. But what must transpire for these important lessons to be learned? Sometimes: conflict! In a cycle guided by the number 2, we'll find ourselves in more situations that require healthy emotional detachment. This is a year to back off from our own staunch viewpoints. Seeing all sides of the equation helps us formulate win-win scenarios rather than win-lose outcomes.

Humble thyself. Working with Master numbers is a marathon, not a sprint. We have to train, be flexible and take the tough coaching. Rushing into anything will lead to burnout. Master numbers teach us humility. We must overcome ego and connect with a deep sense of service before we can truly manifest the power of 11. ✳

Felicia Bender, Ph.D.—The Practical Numerologist— is Astrostyle's resident numerologist and author of *Redesign Your Life: Using Numerology to Create the Wildly Optimal You.* Follow her at www.FeliciaBender.com

The AstroTwins' 2018 Gemini Planetary Planner

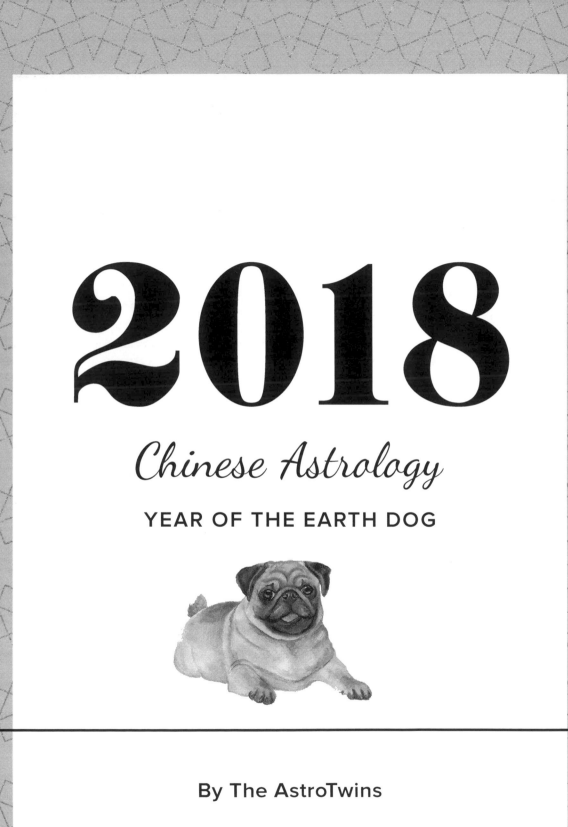

2018

Chinese Astrology

YEAR OF THE EARTH DOG

By The AstroTwins

2018 Chinese Horoscope:

YEAR OF THE EARTH DOG

Let's hear it for #PackGoals! Teamwork makes the dream work in 2018 as the loyal, hardworking Earth Dog takes the wheel on February 15. After an exhausting year of hustling under the manic Fire Rooster's command, who couldn't use an extra set of claws and paws? In 2018, we'll get by with a little help from our friends. The question is, who will pass the strict inner circle criteria that the cosmic canine demands? Loyalty will be the new "L-word" during this Earth Dog year, and points must be earned through authentic allegiance. (Frisky tail wags, gleaming coats and bared teeth notwithstanding.)

Mark your turf—but play well with others.

Dog years can make everyone a lot more territorial, and having a safe haven to call our own is a must in 2018. Home sales (and prices) will continue to trend up in many markets—and, by extension, so will the popularity of shelter blogs, home décor shows and Instagram interior decorators. Gotta customize the doghouse—and make sure everyone knows that it's yours, right? With the earth element ruling in 2018, go green with your selections. Now's the time for owners to invest in renewable energy solutions like solar and wind. Planting gardens and trees can also cleanse the air while improving curb appeal.

With xenophobia on the rise, however, this

What's Your Chinese Zodiac Sign?

Rat: 1924, 1936, 1948, 1960, 1972, 1984, 1996, 2008
Ox: 1925, 1937, 1949, 1961, 1973, 1985, 1997, 2009
Tiger: 1926, 1938, 1950, 1962, 1974, 1986, 1998, 2010
Rabbit: 1927, 1939, 1951, 1963, 1975, 1987, 1999, 2011
Dragon: 1928, 1940, 1952, 1964, 1976, 1988, 2000, 2012
Snake: 1929, 1941, 1953, 1965, 1977, 1989, 2001, 2013
Horse: 1930, 1942, 1954, 1966, 1978, 1990, 2002, 2014
Sheep: 1931, 1943, 1955, 1967, 1979, 1991, 2003, 2015
Monkey: 1932, 1944, 1956, 1968, 1980, 1992, 2004, 2016
Rooster: 1933, 1945, 1957, 1969, 1981, 1993, 2005, 2017
Dog: 1934, 1946, 1958, 1970, 1982, 1994, 2006, 2018
Pig: 1935, 1947, 1959, 1971, 1983, 1995, 2007, 2019

The AstroTwins' 2018 Gemini Planetary Planner

> "Insta-BFFs and Facebook faux-friending will go the way of the dinosaur in 2018. As anyone who has unleashed their pet at a dog park can attest, canines have a systematic getting-to-know-you process."

border patrolling can be a double-edged sword. As protective pups bark at any rando who crosses our property line, we can also grow unnecessarily suspicious of our good-willed neighbors. The challenge in 2018 will be setting healthy boundaries without erecting immovable walls.

That said, the world *can* be a dangerous place and the question remains: How on-guard do we legit need to be? The Dog has an idea: Put people through the sniff test before allowing them into your pack. Insta-BFFs and Facebook faux-friending will go the way of the dinosaur in 2018. As anyone who has unleashed their pet at a dog

park can attest, canines have a systematic getting-to-know-you process. Before they romp and play, they bark at each other, growl and, yes, get a whiff of each other's most private parts.

Metaphorically, the Year of the Earth Dog requires a similar meet-and-greet strategy. Can we open up and show our most vulnerable sides to each other? That level of transparency could be considered crass, but in 2018, being "too real" can be a huge trust-builder. It's kind of like the children's book *Everyone Poops*, which was written with the intent of normalizing a bodily function that's considered rather embarrassing—unless, of course, you're a dog. This creature's excretory habits are the most publicly observed and accepted. While we're not suggesting you cop a squat on a city sidewalk, 2018 is the year for people to get honest and stop acting like their s**t don't stink.

Keep calm and canine on.

More than almost any other emotion, dogs have a keen ability to sense fear. And during the Year of the Earth Dog, we can be easily riled, especially in the face of uncertainty. Politicians, bullies, and even trusted media sources that rely on clicks for revenue, can rile up the fear factor. A sanity saver? Create a grounding practice that utilizes the earth element. This can be as basic as a 30-minute morning walk or leaning against a tall tree for its stalwart support.

Dial down angst-inducing stimulants like caffeine and sugar, and reach for natural snacks like raw nuts, apple wedges and healthy proteins. Turn off news alerts and only check world events at set times so you aren't sent into a panic spiral every time a "breaking headline" posts. Bring this

76

digital detox to your bedroom and invest in a legit alarm clock instead of sleeping with your mobile phone on your nightstand.

Alpha males and tough bitches.

As the Year of the Fire Cock turns over to the Year of the Earth Dog, will we see more Alpha male antics? Ugh, we're afraid so. We have one more year of law and order ideology and scary dog-whistling politics to weather before the hedonistic Earth Boar shakes it up in 2019.

But 2018 comes with a warning label: Don't mess with the bitches! The Dog is associated with Western astrology's Libra, the sign of equality and justice. The age-old, imbalanced power dynamics between men and women will continue to raise hackles in 2018. Domineering types who use their stature to intimidate, control and abuse the pack could be locked out of the doghouse (and perhaps penned up in the Big House). The feminist revolution of 2018 might even reclaim the word "bitch" (perhaps bedazzled on a choker) as the upleveled pussy hat. Designers, you heard it here first.

Fierce & furry: fashion in the Year of the Dog.

On that note, dig out your poodle skirt! Fido-fierce fashion could find its way to the glossy mags in 2018—and with a "best in show" twist. Scorpio RuPaul already has Jupiter on his side this year, but the runway competitions could grow to insane proportions. With Jupiter in Scorpio, fetishwear is already making a comeback. A haute harness could replace the corset belt as a way to dress up denim along with collar-style necklaces and studded leather accents. Coats with curly faux fur will also remain on-trend. Shiny, glossy finishes may dominate beauty blogs from nails to lips to tresses. Curly hair, don't care? The "poodle pouf" could put a fresh spin on the faux-hawk in 2018.

Relationships get strong and stable.

Dog years can be stabilizing for relationships, as the association with marriage-minded Libra will put folks in a mate-for-life mindset. Heavy petting, anyone? "I need more affection" may be a common cry in 2018. Couples should slow down and reconnect through touch. Single? You could find love through a pack-mate's introduction, so don't skip out on the group hangs. Tinder and dating apps could take a backseat to IRL meetups. During Dog years, body language and chemistry (yep, those pheromones are real) are the true litmus test—and can't be sensed on screen.

While Jupiter in Scorpio will expedite detective work, should we let sleeping dogs lie? Digging is a Dog year tendency, but one that can open Pandora's box. Some bones are best left buried, especially if matters were resolved long ago. But if you need to excavate during this Earth Dog year, be prepared to discover more than you bargained for hidden below the crust. Old cases may be reopened as new evidence is submitted. Toto, we are not in Kansas anymore.

"Since the zodiac's Dog is associated with diplomatic Libra, this is the year to adopt a peaceful approach to conflict resolution."

Work hard, play hard.

Daily play breaks are a must in the Year of the Mutt—the more physical the better. But don't expect to snuff out the midnight oil lamp when you get back from your run through the park. The Earth Dog needs creature comforts and is willing to work hard for them. With partnership-oriented Libra being the Western celestial signature for the Pooch, joint ventures are the best way to avoid workaholism and win all the toys. The sharing economy, like ride pools and coworking offices, will continue to flourish in 2018.

Clever communication ruled the day under the Rooster's reign, but the Dog declares a ceasefire to the 2017 Twitter wars. It's bittersweet, since the cocky Fire Rooster raised #hashtag humor to a whole new level. But in the end, those constant clapbacks only escalated the battle. Doggie-style discussions are far more basic. Think: simple commands uttered in an authoritative tone of voice.

Body language will speak volumes, too. TV's Cesar Milan, a.k.a. The Dog Whisperer, underscored the importance of a "calm-assertive" demeanor as the key to keeping unruly canines in check. In 2018, you can work the room like Milan in a pack of pit bulls. Instead of racking your brain for a snappy comeback, strengthen your posture.

Increase the peace!

Since the zodiac's Dog is associated with diplomatic Libra, this is the year to adopt a peaceful approach to conflict resolution. And what's the best way to reinforce good behavior in dogs, and yes, humans? Not shouting or spanking them with a newspaper or locking them up in a small space. That just makes them sneaky, scared and ferocious.

Instead, opt for praise and positive reinforcement (along with that posture). Lead with compliments and be very vocal when you're happy with the way things are going. ("Who's a good boyyyyyy?!") Buffer critiques in a "praise sandwich," starting and ending with an acknowledgment and slipping feedback in between like a creamy filling—or maybe a heartworm pill wrapped in a slice of deli meat.

By acknowledging the good in others, we might just stand a chance at world peace in 2018. Now, who wants a cookie? ✳

PLAN IT BY THE PLANETS!

2018

Cosmic Calendar

DAILY PLANETARY GUIDE

January 2018

01 MON

○ Cancer full moon (supermoon) 9:24pm EST

02 TUE

03 WED

04 THU

05 FRI

06 SAT

Mars conjunct Jupiter (Scorpio)
Uranus D in Aries

07 SUN

January 2018

08 MON

◐   Libra 3rd quarter moon

09 TUE

Sun conjunct Pluto (Capricorn)
Sun conjunct Venus (Capricorn)
Venus conjunct Pluto (Capricorn)

10 WED

11 THU

Mercury enters Capricorn

12 FRI

13 SAT

Venus (Capricorn) square Uranus (Aries)

14 SUN

Sun (Capricorn) square Uranus (Aries)

January 2018

15 MON ───────────────────────────

16 TUE ───────────────────────────

● Capricorn new moon 9:17pm EST

17 WED ───────────────────────────

Venus enters Aquarius

18 THU ───────────────────────────

19 FRI ───────────────────────────

Sun enters Aquarius

20 SAT ───────────────────────────

21 SUN ───────────────────────────

January 2018

22 MON

23 TUE

24 WED

◑ Taurus 1st quarter moon

25 THU

26 FRI

Mars enters Sagittarius

27 SAT

28 SUN

The AstroTwins' 2018 Gemini Planetary Planner

January 2018

29 MON ————————————————————————————————————

30 TUE ————————————————————————————————————

31 WED ————————————————————————————————————

Mercury enters Aquarius

○ Leo full moon (total lunar eclipse & supermoon) 8:26am EST

JAN	S	M	T	W	T	F	S
		1	2	3	4	5	6
	7	8	9	10	11	12	13
	14	15	16	17	18	19	20
	21	22	23	24	25	26	27
	28	29	30	31			

FEB	S	M	T	W	T	F	S
					1	2	3
	4	5	6	7	8	9	10
	11	12	13	14	15	16	17
	18	19	20	21	22	23	24
	25	26	27	28			

MAR	S	M	T	W	T	F	S
					1	2	3
	4	5	6	7	8	9	10
	11	12	13	14	15	16	17
	18	19	20	21	22	23	24
	25	26	27	28	29	30	

February 2018

———————————————————————————————— 01 THU

———————————————————————————————— 02 FRI

———————————————————————————————— 03 SAT

———————————————————————————————— 04 SUN

Venus (Aquarius) square Jupiter (Scorpio)

———————————————————————————————— 05 MON

———————————————————————————————— 06 TUE

———————————————————————————————— 07 WED

◑ Scorpio 3rd quarter moon

     The AstroTwins' 2018 Gemini Planetary Planner

February 2018

08 THU

09 FRI

10 SAT

Venus enters Pisces

Sun (Aquarius) square Jupiter (Scorpio)

11 SUN

12 MON

13 TUE

14 WED

February 2018

--- **15 THU**

● Aquarius new moon (partial solar eclipse) 4:05pm EST

Chinese New Year (Year of the Earth Dog)

--- **16 FRI**

--- **17 SAT**

Mercury enters Pisces

Mars (Sagittarius) square Neptune (Pisces)

--- **18 SUN**

Sun enters Pisces

--- **19 MON**

--- **20 TUE**

--- **21 WED**

Venus conjunct Neptune (Pisces)

87   The AstroTwins' 2018 Gemini Planetary Planner

February 2018

22 THU ───────────────────────────────────────

23 FRI ───────────────────────────────────────

◐ Gemini 1st quarter moon

24 SAT ───────────────────────────────────────

25 SUN ───────────────────────────────────────

Venus (Pisces) square Mars (Sagittarius)

26 MON ───────────────────────────────────────

27 TUE ─────────────────────── **28 WED** ───────────────────

FEB	S	M	T	W	T	F	S
					1	2	3
	4	5	6	7	8	9	10
	11	12	13	14	15	16	17
	18	19	20	21	22	23	24
	25	26	27	28			

MAR	S	M	T	W	T	F	S
					1	2	3
	4	5	6	7	8	9	10
	11	12	13	14	15	16	17
	18	19	20	21	22	23	24
	25	26	27	28	29	30	

APR	S	M	T	W	T	F	S
	1	2	3	4	5	6	7
	8	9	10	11	12	13	14
	15	16	17	18	19	20	21
	22	23	24	25	26	27	28
	29	30					

88

March 2018

01 THU

○ Virgo full moon 7:51pm

Venus (Pisces) trine Jupiter (Scorpio)

02 FRI

03 SAT

04 SUN

Sun conjunct Neptune (Pisces)

05 MON

06 TUE

Mercury enters Aries

Venus enters Aries

07 WED

The AstroTwins' 2018 Gemini Planetary Planner

March 2018

08 THU

Jupiter Rx in Scorpio

09 FRI

◑ Sagittarius 3rd quarter moon

10 SAT

11 SUN

Mars (Sagittarius) trine Uranus (Aries)

12 MON

13 TUE

Sun (Pisces) trine Jupiter (Scorpio)

Venus (Aries) square Saturn (Capricorn)

14 WED

90

March 2018

15 THU

16 FRI

17 SAT

● Pisces new moon 9:11am

Mars enters Capricorn

18 SUN

19 MON

20 TUE

Sun enters Aries

21 WED

March 2018

22 THU ——————————————————————————

Mercury Rx in Aries

23 FRI ——————————————————————————

Venus (Aries) square Pluto (Capricorn)

24 SAT ——————————————————————————

◗   Cancer 1st quarter moon

Sun (Aries) square Mars (Capricorn)

25 SUN ——————————————————————————

26 MON ——————————————————————————

27 TUE ——————————————————————————

28 WED ——————————————————————————

Venus conjunct Uranus (Aries)

March 2018

---

29 THU

Sun (Aries) square Saturn (Capricorn)

---

30 FRI

---

31 SAT

◯ Libra full moon 8:36am EST

Venus enters Taurus

MAR	S	M	T	W	T	F	S
					1	2	3
	4	5	6	7	8	9	10
	11	12	13	14	15	16	17
	18	19	20	21	22	23	24
	25	26	27	28	29	30	

APR	S	M	T	W	T	F	S
	1	2	3	4	5	6	7
	8	9	10	11	12	13	14
	15	16	17	18	19	20	21
	22	23	24	25	26	27	28
	29	30					

MAY	S	M	T	W	T	F	S
			1	2	3	4	5
	6	7	8	9	10	11	12
	13	14	15	16	17	18	19
	20	21	22	23	24	25	26
	27	28	29	30	31		

April 2018

01 SUN ——————————————————————————————————————

02 MON ——————————————————————————————————————

Mars conjunct Saturn (Capricorn)

03 TUE ——————————————————————————————————————

04 WED ——————————————————————————————————————

05 THU ——————————————————————————————————————

06 FRI ———————————————————————————————————————

07 SAT ———————————————————————————————————————

Venus (Taurus) trine Saturn (Capricorn)

April 2018

08 SUN

◑ Capricorn 3rd quarter moon

09 MON

10 TUE

11 WED

Sun (Aries) square Pluto (Capricorn)

Venus (Taurus) trine Mars (Capricorn)

12 THU

13 FRI

14 SAT

 The AstroTwins' 2018 Gemini Planetary Planner

April 2018

15 SUN

● Aries new moon 9:57pm

Mercury direct in Aries

16 MON

17 TUE

Saturn Rx in Capricorn

Venus (Taurus) opposite Jupiter (Scorpio)

Venus (Taurus) trine Pluto (Capricorn)

18 WED

Sun conjunct Uranus (Aries)

19 THU

Sun enters Taurus

20 FRI

21 SAT

96

April 2018

22 SUN

Pluto Rx in Capricorn

◐ Leo 1st quarter moon

23 MON

24 TUE

Venus enters Gemini

25 WED

26 THU

Mars conjunct Pluto (Capricorn)

27 FRI

28 SAT

The AstroTwins' 2018 Gemini Planetary Planner

April 2018

29 SUN

◯ Scorpio full moon 8:58pm EST

Sun (Taurus) trine Saturn (Capricorn)

30 MON

	S	M	T	W	T	F	S
APR	1	2	3	4	5	6	7
	8	9	10	11	12	13	14
	15	16	17	18	19	20	21
	22	23	24	25	26	27	28
	29	30					

	S	M	T	W	T	F	S
MAY			1	2	3	4	5
	6	7	8	9	10	11	12
	13	14	15	16	17	18	19
	20	21	22	23	24	25	26
	27	28	29	30	31		

	S	M	T	W	T	F	S
JUN						1	2
	3	4	5	6	7	8	9
	10	11	12	13	14	15	16
	17	18	19	20	21	22	23
	24	25	26	27	28	29	30

May 2018

01 TUE

02 WED

03 THU

04 FRI

05 SAT

06 SUN

07 MON

◑ Aquarius 3rd quarter moon

Venus (Gemini) square Neptune (Pisces)

     The AstroTwins' 2018 Gemini Planetary Planner

May 2018

08 TUE ——————————————————————————————

Sun (Taurus) opposite Jupiter (Scorpio)

09 WED ——————————————————————————————

10 THU ——————————————————————————————

11 FRI ——————————————————————————————

Sun (Taurus) trine Pluto (Capricorn)

12 SAT ——————————————————————————————

13 SUN ——————————————————————————————

Mercury enters Taurus

14 MON ——————————————————————————————

May 2018

15 TUE

● Taurus new moon 7:47am EST

Uranus enters Taurus (until November 6)

16 WED

Mars enters Aquarius

Mars (Aquarius) square Uranus (Taurus)

17 THU

18 FRI

19 SAT

Venus enters Cancer

20 SUN

Sun enters Gemini

21 MON

◑ Virgo 1st quarter moon

The AstroTwins' 2018 Gemini Planetary Planner

May 2018

22 TUE ────────────────────────────────

23 WED ────────────────────────────────

Sun (Gemini) trine Mars (Aquarius)

24 THU ────────────────────────────────

25 FRI ────────────────────────────────

Jupiter (Scorpio) trine Neptune (Pisces)

26 SAT ────────────────────────────────

Venus (Cancer) opposite Saturn (Capricorn)

27 SUN ────────────────────────────────

28 MON ────────────────────────────────

May 2018

29 TUE

○ Sagittarius full moon 10:19am EST

Mercury enters Gemini

30 WED

31 THU

MAY	S	M	T	W	T	F	S
			1	2	3	4	5
	6	7	8	9	10	11	12
	13	14	15	16	17	18	19
	20	21	22	23	24	25	26
	27	28	29	30	31		

JUN	S	M	T	W	T	F	S
						1	2
	3	4	5	6	7	8	9
	10	11	12	13	14	15	16
	17	18	19	20	21	22	23
	24	25	26	27	28	29	30

JUL	S	M	T	W	T	F	S
	1	2	3	4	5	6	7
	8	9	10	11	12	13	14
	15	16	17	18	19	20	21
	22	23	24	25	26	27	28
	29	30	31				

June 2018

01 FRI

Venus (Cancer) trine Jupiter (Scorpio)

02 SAT

Venus (Cancer) trine Neptune (Pisces)

03 SUN

04 MON

05 TUE

Venus (Cancer) opposite Pluto (Capricorn)

06 WED

◐   Pisces 3rd quarter moon

07 THU

Sun (Gemini) square Neptune (Pisces)

June 2018

08 FRI

09 SAT

10 SUN

11 MON

12 TUE

Mercury enters Cancer

13 WED

● Gemini new moon 3:43pm EST

Venus enters Leo

14 THU

Venus (Leo) square Uranus (Taurus)

The AstroTwins' 2018 Gemini Planetary Planner

June 2018

15 FRI ───────────────────────────────

16 SAT ───────────────────────────────

17 SUN ───────────────────────────────

18 MON ───────────────────────────────

Neptune Rx in Pisces

19 TUE ───────────────────────────────

20 WED ───────────────────────────────

◑ Virgo 1st quarter moonn

21 THU ───────────────────────────────

Sun enters Cancer

Venus (Leo) opposite Mars (Aquarius)

The AstroTwins' 2018 Gemini Planetary Planner   106

June 2018

_____ **22 FRI**

_____ **23 SAT**

_____ **24 SUN**

_____ **25 MON**

Venus (Leo) square Jupiter (Scorpio)

_____ **26 TUE**

Mars Rx in Aquarius

_____ **27 WED**

Sun (Cancer) opposite Saturn (Capricorn)

_____ **28 THU**

○ Capricorn full moon 12:53am

107 The AstroTwins' 2018 Gemini Planetary Planner

June 2018

29 FRI _____

Mercury enters Leo

30 SAT _____

	S	M	T	W	T	F	S
MAY			1	2	3	4	5
	6	7	8	9	10	11	12
	13	14	15	16	17	18	19
	20	21	22	23	24	25	26
	27	28	29	30	31		

	S	M	T	W	T	F	S
JUN						1	2
	3	4	5	6	7	8	9
	10	11	12	13	14	15	16
	17	18	19	20	21	22	23
	24	25	26	27	28	29	30

	S	M	T	W	T	F	S
JUL	1	2	3	4	5	6	7
	8	9	10	11	12	13	14
	15	16	17	18	19	20	21
	22	23	24	25	26	27	28
	29	30	31				

July 2018

01 SUN

02 MON

03 TUE

04 WED

05 THU

Sun (Cancer) trine Jupiter (Scorpio)

06 FRI

◐ Aries 3rd quarter moon

07 SAT

 The AstroTwins' 2018 Gemini Planetary Planner

July 2018

08 SUN

Sun (Cancer) trine Neptune (Pisces)

09 MON

Venus enters Virgo

10 TUE

Jupiter D in Scorpio

11 WED

Venus (Virgo) trine Uranus (Taurus)

12 THU

● Cancer new moon (partial solar eclipse) 10:47pm EST

Sun (Cancer) opposite Pluto (Capricorn)

13 FRI

14 SAT

Venus (Virgo) trine Saturn (Capricorn)

110

July 2018

15 SUN

16 MON

17 TUE

18 WED

19 THU

◑ Libra 1st quarter moon

20 FRI

21 SAT

The AstroTwins' 2018 Gemini Planetary Planner

July 2018

22 SUN

Sun enters Leo

23 MON

24 TUE

Venus (Virgo) opposite Neptune (Pisces)

25 WED

Sun (Leo) square Uranus (Taurus)

26 THU

Mercury retrograde in Leo

27 FRI

○ Aquarius full moon (total lunar eclipse) 4:20pm EST

Sun (Leo) opposite Mars (Aquarius)

Venus (Virgo) trine Pluto (Capricorn)

28 SAT

112

July 2018

29 SUN

30 MON

31 TUE

	S	M	T	W	T	F	S
						1	2
JUN	3	4	5	6	7	8	9
	10	11	12	13	14	15	16
	17	18	19	20	21	22	23
	24	25	26	27	28	29	30

	S	M	T	W	T	F	S
	1	2	3	4	5	6	7
JUL	8	9	10	11	12	13	14
	15	16	17	18	19	20	21
	22	23	24	25	26	27	28
	29	30	31				

	S	M	T	W	T	F	S
				1	2	3	4
AUG	5	6	7	8	9	10	11
	12	13	14	15	16	17	18
	19	20	21	22	23	24	25
	26	27	28	29	30	31	

August 2018

01 WED ——————————————————————————————————

02 THU ——————————————————————————————————

Mars (Aquarius) square Uranus (Taurus)

03 FRI ——————————————————————————————————

04 SAT ——————————————————————————————————

◑   Taurus 3rd quarter moon

05 SUN ——————————————————————————————————

06 MON ——————————————————————————————————

Venus enters Libra

Sun (Leo) square Jupiter (Scorpio)

07 TUE ——————————————————————————————————

Uranus Rx in Taurus

Venus (Libra) trine Mars (Aquarius)

....

August 2018

08 WED

09 THU

Venus (Libra) square Saturn (Capricorn)

10 FRI

11 SAT

● Leo new moon (partial solar eclipse) 5:57am EST

12 SUN

Mars Rx into Capricorn

13 MON

14 TUE

The AstroTwins' 2018 Gemini Planetary Planner

August 2018

15 WED ――――――――――――――――――――――――――――

16 THU ――――――――――――――――――――――――――――

17 FRI ――――――――――――――――――――――――――――

18 SAT ――――――――――――――――――――――――――――

◑   Scorpio 1st quarter moon

19 SUN ――――――――――――――――――――――――――――

Mercury Direct in Leo

Jupiter (Scorpio) trine Neptune (Pisces)

20 MON ――――――――――――――――――――――――――――

21 TUE ――――――――――――――――――――――――――――

The AstroTwins' 2018 Gemini Planetary Planner   116

August 2018

——————————————————————————————————— **22 WED**

——————————————————————————————————— **23 THU**

Sun enters Virgo

——————————————————————————————————— **24 FRI**

——————————————————————————————————— **25 SAT**

Sun (Virgo) trine Uranus (Taurus)

Sun (Virgo) trine Saturn (Capricorn)

——————————————————————————————————— **26 SUN**

◯ Pisces full moon 7:56am EST

Venus (Libra) square Pluto (Capricorn)

——————————————————————————————————— **27 MON**

Mars D in Capricorn

——————————————————————————————————— **28 TUE**

August 2018

29 WED

30 THU

31 FRI

	S	M	T	W	T	F	S
		1	2	3	4	5	6	7
JUL	8	9	10	11	12	13	14
	15	16	17	18	19	20	21
	22	23	24	25	26	27	28
	29	30	31				

	S	M	T	W	T	F	S
				1	2	3	4
AUG	5	6	7	8	9	10	11
	12	13	14	15	16	17	18
	19	20	21	22	23	24	25
	26	27	28	29	30	31	

	S	M	T	W	T	F	S
							1
SEP	2	3	4	5	6	7	8
	9	10	11	12	13	14	15
	16	17	18	19	20	21	22
	23	24	25	26	27	28	29
	30						

The AstroTwins' 2018 Gemini Planetary Planner   118

September 2018

01 SAT

02 SUN

◐ Gemini 3rd quarter moon

03 MON

04 TUE

05 WED

Mercury enters Virgo (until 9/22)

06 THU

Saturn direct in Capricorn

07 FRI

Sun (Virgo) opposite Neptune (Pisces)

September 2018

08 SAT

Venus (Libra) square Mars (Capricorn)

09 SUN

● Virgo new moon 2:01pm EST

Venus enters Scorpio

10 MON

Mars enters Aquarius

11 TUE

Sun (Virgo) trine Pluto (Capricorn)

12 WED

Venus (Scorpio) opposite Uranus (Taurus)

13 THU

14 FRI

September 2018

15 SAT

16 SUN

◐ Sagittarius 1st quarter moon

17 MON

18 TUE

Mars (Aquarius) square Uranus (Taurus)

19 WED

20 THU

21 FRI

Mercury enters Libra

September 2018

22 SAT

Sun enters Libra

23 SUN

24 MON

○ Aries full moon 10:52pm EST

25 TUE

Sun (Libra) square Saturn (Capricorn)

26 WED

27 THU

Sun (Libra) trine Mars (Aquarius)

28 FRI

September 2018

29 SAT

30 SUN

Pluto direct in Capricorn

	S	M	T	W	T	F	S
AUG				1	2	3	4
	5	6	7	8	9	10	11
	12	13	14	15	16	17	18
	19	20	21	22	23	24	25
	26	27	28	29	30	31	

	S	M	T	W	T	F	S
SEP							1
	2	3	4	5	6	7	8
	9	10	11	12	13	14	15
	16	17	18	19	20	21	22
	23	24	25	26	27	28	29
	30						

	S	M	T	W	T	F	S
OCT		1	2	3	4	5	6
	7	8	9	10	11	12	13
	14	15	16	17	18	19	20
	21	22	23	24	25	26	27
	28	29	30	31			

The AstroTwins' 2018 Gemini Planetary Planner

October 2018

01 MON ────────────────────────────────

02 TUE ────────────────────────────────

◑ Cancer 3rd quarter moon

03 WED ────────────────────────────────

04 THU ────────────────────────────────

05 FRI ────────────────────────────────

Venus Rx in Scorpio

06 SAT ────────────────────────────────

07 SUN ────────────────────────────────

October 2018

08 MON

● Libra new moon 11:46pm EST

09 TUE

Mercury in Scorpio

10 WED

Venus (Scorpio) square Mars (Aquarius)

11 THU

12 FRI

Sun (Libra) square Pluto (Capricorn)

13 SAT

14 SUN

The AstroTwins' 2018 Gemini Planetary Planner

October 2018

15 MON ————————————————————————————————

16 TUE ————————————————————————————————

◑ Capricorn 1st quarter moon

17 WED ————————————————————————————————

18 THU ————————————————————————————————

19 FRI ————————————————————————————————

20 SAT ————————————————————————————————

21 SUN ————————————————————————————————

126

October 2018

22 MON

---

23 TUE

Sun enters Scorpio

---

24 WED

○ Taurus full moon 12:45pm EST

Sun (Scorpio) opposite Uranus (Taurus)

---

25 THU

---

26 FRI

Sun conjunct Venus (Scorpio)

---

27 SAT

---

28 SUN

October 2018

29 MON

30 TUE

31 WED

◐ Leo 3rd quarter moon

Mercury enters Sagittarius

Venus Rx into Libra

Venus (Scorpio) opposite Uranus (Taurus)

	S	M	T	W	T	F	S
							1
SEP	2	3	4	5	6	7	8
	9	10	11	12	13	14	15
	16	17	18	19	20	21	22
	23	24	25	26	27	28	29
	30						

	S	M	T	W	T	F	S
		1	2	3	4	5	6
OCT	7	8	9	10	11	12	13
	14	15	16	17	18	19	20
	21	22	23	24	25	26	27
	28	29	30	31			

	S	M	T	W	T	F	S
					1	2	3
NOV	4	5	6	7	8	9	10
	11	12	13	14	15	16	17
	18	19	20	21	22	23	24
	25	26	27	28	29	30	

November 2018

——————————————————————————————————————— 01 THU

——————————————————————————————————————— 02 FRI

——————————————————————————————————————— 03 SAT

——————————————————————————————————————— 04 SUN

——————————————————————————————————————— 05 MON

——————————————————————————————————————— 06 TUE

Uranus Rx into Aries

——————————————————————————————————————— 07 WED

● Scorpio new moon 11:01am EST

       The AstroTwins' 2018 Gemini Planetary Planner

November 2018

08 THU

Jupiter enters Sagittarius

09 FRI

Venus (Libra) trine Mars (Aquarius)

10 SAT

11 SUN

12 MON

13 TUE

14 WED

The AstroTwins' 2018 Gemini Planetary Planner   130

November 2018

15 THU

Mars enters Pisces

Aquarius 1st quarter moon

16 FRI

Venus direct in Libra

Mercury Rx in Sagittarius

17 SAT

18 SUN

19 MON

Mars (Pisces) square Jupiter (Sagittarius)

20 TUE

21 WED

The AstroTwins' 2018 Gemini Planetary Planner

November 2018

22 THU

Sun enters Sagittarius

23 FRI

○ Gemini full moon 12:30am EST

24 SAT

Neptune direct in Pisces

25 SUN

26 MON

Sun conjunct Jupiter (Sagittarius)

27 TUE

28 WED

132

November 2018

29 THU

◑ Virgo 3rd quarter moon

30 FRI

Venus (Libra) opposite Uranus (Aries)

	S	M	T	W	T	F	S
		1	2	3	4	5	6
OCT	7	8	9	10	11	12	13
	14	15	16	17	18	19	20
	21	22	23	24	25	26	27
	28	29	30	31			

	S	M	T	W	T	F	S
					1	2	3
NOV	4	5	6	7	8	9	10
	11	12	13	14	15	16	17
	18	19	20	21	22	23	24
	25	26	27	28	29	30	

	S	M	T	W	T	F	S
							1
DEC	2	3	4	5	6	7	8
	9	10	11	12	13	14	15
	16	17	18	19	20	21	22
	23	24	25	26	27	28	29
	30	31					

The AstroTwins' 2018 Gemini Planetary Planner

December 2018

01 SAT —————————————————————————————————

Mercury Rx into Scorpio

02 SUN —————————————————————————————————

Venus enters Scorpio

Sun (Sagittarius) square Mars (Pisces)

03 MON —————————————————————————————————

04 TUE —————————————————————————————————

05 WED —————————————————————————————————

Sun (Sagittarius) square Neptune (Pisces)

06 THU —————————————————————————————————

Mercury direct in Scorpio

07 FRI —————————————————————————————————

● Sagittarius new moon 2:20am EST

Mars conjunct Neptune (Pisces)

134

December 2018

08 SAT

09 SUN

10 MON

11 TUE

12 WED

Mercury enters Sagittarius

13 THU

14 FRI

The AstroTwins' 2018 Gemini Planetary Planner

December 2018

15 SAT

◑ Pisces 1st quarter moon

16 SUN

17 MON

18 TUE

19 WED

20 THU

Sun (Sagittarius) trine Uranus (Aries)

21 FRI

Sun enters Capricorn

Venus (Scorpio) trine Neptune (Pisces)

The AstroTwins' 2018 Gemini Planetary Planner   136

December 2018

_____ **22 SAT**

○ Cancer full moon 12:48pm EST

_____ **23 SUN**

_____ **24 MON**

_____ **25 TUE**

_____ **26 WED**

_____ **27 THU**

_____ **28 FRI**

December 2018

29 SAT

◑ Libra 3rd quarter moon

30 SUN

31 MON

	S	M	T	W	T	F	S
NOV					1	2	3
	4	5	6	7	8	9	10
	11	12	13	14	15	16	17
	18	19	20	21	22	23	24
	25	26	27	28	29	30	

	S	M	T	W	T	F	S
DEC							1
	2	3	4	5	6	7	8
	9	10	11	12	13	14	15
	16	17	18	19	20	21	22
	23	24	25	26	27	28	29
	30	31					

	S	M	T	W	T	F	S
JAN			1	2	3	4	5
	6	7	8	9	10	11	12
	13	14	15	16	17	18	19
	20	21	22	23	24	25	26
	27	28	29	30	31		

The AstroTwins' 2018 Gemini Planetary Planner   138

Ophira & Tali Edut

Dubbed the "astrologers to the stars," identical twin sisters Ophira and Tali Edut, known as the AstroTwins, are professional astrologers who reach millions worldwide through their spot-on predictions. Through their website, Astrostyle. com, Ophira and Tali help "bring the stars down to earth" with their unique, lifestyle-based approach to astrology. They are also the official astrologers for Refinery29, ELLE.com, *ELLE* Magazine (U.S.) and MindBodyGreen.com. The AstroTwins have been featured in the the New York *Times* and *People* and they've collaborated with major brands including Vogue, Nordstrom, Revlon, H&M, Urban Outfitters, Ted Baker and Kate Spade.

The sisters have read charts for celebrities including Beyoncé, Stevie Wonder, Emma Roberts, Karlie Kloss and Sting. They are regular guests on SiriusXM and have appeared on Bravo's *The Real Housewives of New Jersey*, doing on-air readings for the cast. They have authored four print books: *AstroStyle, Love Zodiac, Shoestrology* and *Momstrology* (their #1 Amazon best-selling astrological parenting guide) and a growing collection of ebooks, including their popular annual horoscope guides. ✳

VISIT THE ASTROTWINS AT WWW.ASTROSTYLE.COM
Follow us on social media @astrotwins

This year's edition is dedicated with infinite love and appreciation to our aunt Carolyn Mickelson (Oon), our sister-friend Tansy Stowell and our beloved dachshund Seymour. You are with us always.

♡